"Checkpoint!" the driver cried.

The taxi slowed as it reached the barricade, and the harsh glare of a searchlight spilled into the interior, revealing Sigourney's companion at last. His lean profile suggested he was a man of experience. He was gorgeous—and slightly dangerous, too. Yet somehow she knew he meant her no harm.

"If they ask, we're newlyweds on our honeymoon," he ordered. Then he surprised her by drawing her arms around his rib cage. With a shock she felt the knife sheathed under his left arm. The second shock came when he bent his head and kissed her.

Dear Reader,

When two people fall in love, the world is suddenly new and exciting, and it's that same excitement we bring to you in Silhouette Intimate Moments. These are stories with scope, with grandeur. These characters lead the lives we all dream of, and everything they do reflects the wonder of being in love.

Longer and more sensuous than most romances, Silhouette Intimate Moments novels take you away from everyday life and let you share the magic of love. Adventure, glamour, drama, even suspense— these are the passwords that let you into a world where love has a power beyond the ordinary, where the best authors in the field today create stories of love and commitment that will stay with you always.

In coming months look for novels by your favorite authors: Maura Seger, Parris Afton Bonds, Elizabeth Lowell and Erin St. Claire, to name just a few. And whenever you buy books, look for all the Silhouette Intimate Moments, love stories *for* today's women *by* today's women.

Leslie J. Wainger
Senior Editor
Silhouette Books

IMRL-7/85

Midsummer Midnight

Parris Afton Bonds

Silhouette Intimate Moments

Published by Silhouette Books New York

America's Publisher of Contemporary Romance

SILHOUETTE BOOKS
300 E. 42nd St., New York, N.Y. 10017

Copyright © 1985 by Parris Afton Bonds

Distributed by Pocket Books

ISBN: 0-373-07113-2

First Silhouette Books printing October 1985

10 9 8 7 6 5 4 3 2 1

America's Publisher of Contemporary Romance

Printed in the U.S.A.

Silhouette Books by Parris Afton Bonds

Silhouette Romance

Made !for Each Other #70

Silhouette Intimate Moments

Wind Song #5
Widow Woman #41
Spinster's Song #77
Midsummer Midnight #113

PARRIS AFTON BONDS

has been writing since she was six, though she didn't turn professional until her family moved to Mexico. She gives the credit for her several literary awards to her husband and sons, who have given unstintingly of their love and support.

For Lois and Ed Nelson—
you make the world a better place.

Chapter 1

Lady Phillipa Fleming replaced the telephone on its cradle and looked at the big Macedonian. His back was to her, but even in the poor light of the apartment she could make out the scars corduroying the flesh that was the color of tobacco leaf. A purple welt furrowed the line of his spine. It was all she could do to repress an urge to run her fingertips along its length.

"The American journalist," she said. "Her flight arrives tonight at 10:05."

He turned from the window to face her. "After curfew, then."

His voice had a deep, richly resonant tone that made one want to hear it again and again. He took the lit cigarette Lady Phillipa held out to him and drew on it, so its flare briefly illuminated his hard, handsome face. The sweetish smell of Turkish tobacco pervaded the small room.

"Will the hour make it difficult?" she said, wondering why she bothered to ask. It seemed to her that he didn't know the meaning of the word difficult. He expected the impossible to happen, and somehow he always seemed to make it do so. It could be frustrating, especially when he also expected the impossible of others.

"The airport taxi will take the road to Old Town," he said, exhaling. "That will be as good a place as any to stop it."

He hadn't answered her question, but then, she should have known he wouldn't.

The electronic glass doors in the Olympia Airways futuristic terminal slid open as if at a silent command, and Sigourney Hamilton hurried through, determined to snare one of the taxis that waited beneath the mercury floodlights beyond. She was exhausted from the transatlantic flight. Forget the round of parties that was to open the mad week of Midsummer Midnight in Constantine. She wanted nothing more than to check in at the hotel and collapse, first in a warm bath and then in a comfortable bed.

In the surge of people, mostly wealthy tourists who flocked to the ancient Macedonian capital, she collided with a grotesquerie dressed all in black.

With quick, self-conscious glances, the passersby assessed him as the ugliest of humans, cursed with a bulbous, veiny nose, a splotched and warted complexion, and a slack, fleshy mouth encompassed by pendulous jowls. The man truly played beast to the stunning beauty of the woman over whom he hulked.

Readjusting the strap of her equipment bag, she pushed back a curtain of blueblack hair and looked up into features that might have terrified someone else. "Father Murphy!" Her smile radiated the profound pleasure she felt at the encounter.

"Sigourney!" The priest enveloped the woman in his meaty arms before releasing her so the two could move out of the flow of scurrying pedestrians. "How long has it been? Five years? Six? What sin or indiscretion brings you to hide out in this misbegotten corner of Europe?"

She had last met the priest when she'd traveled to India to meet with Indira Gandhi. He had been there with the World Health Organization to implement aid for one of Mother Teresa's poverty projects. And before that...twenty-five or so years had intervened. She had been but a child at that first meeting that was to change her life. "The same, as always, Father. An interview."

"Ahh, yes. You're rumored to be something of an international celebrity yourself, you know—with all of the stigmas appropriately attached to the nefarious craft of journalism."

She laughed softly up into the features nature had chosen to curse him with. Her natural zest for life always responded to his dry, lively wit. "Well, you know how it is. Reporting gives me the opportunity to dabble vicariously in delicious sin without having to repent."

"You certainly can't lack for opportunity, my child—not with your blessed face."

"More a lack of imagination on my part."

Within the sunken, rheumy sockets, his intelligent eyes glittered. "It's Agamemnon, isn't it? You're in Constantine to get one of your waspish interviews, and Macedonia's premier is your target."

"You're onto me, Father." Her thumb and fingers fired an imaginary pistol at him. "Another political leader bites the dust!"

His thick, unruly white brows waggled aloft in mock exasperation. "Still speak in italics and exclamation points, do you?" The distorted features drew together as he frowned. "Not here, Sigourney. Your wretched psychojournalism might not escape retribution in Macedonia as easily as you escaped Idi Amin. Got out of Uganda by the hair of your chinny-chin-chin, if I correctly recall the columns of the yellow journalists."

"Don't worry, Father. My American passport is a talisman against tyrants."

"Look, my child, I have a cargo of bibles I've got to pick up here, but tomorrow—"

"Bibles—bahh!" Her pale blue eyes twinkled like distant stars. "More than likely you're picking up a cargo of unconsecrated wine you've smuggled in."

The quivering wattles of his jaw stilled momentarily, and she wondered if the priest was becoming touchier with age. One of the characteristics that had always appealed to her was his unparochial approach to his calling. Abruptly the lugubrious mouth broadened into its genial smile. "Tomorrow, Sigourney, we can meet for lunch at a perfectly salacious taverna I know of. It claims the best *dolmades* in all of Macedonia and a wicked wine, the recipe for which is zealously guarded by the monks of Daphne."

"I have an appointment with General Agamemnon at noon, but I'll meet you afterward. I'm staying at the Acropolis Regency."

Moments later, more than one head turned to watch the woman in white linen slide into the rear seat of the taxi. Her incredible beauty was a gift of her Eurasian heritage—an American father of Greek extraction and a Korean war bride. Their union had created a flawless complexion over scimitar cheekbones, dusky golden skin that appeared to have a perennial tan, dense but vibrant black hair, and thickly lashed almond-shaped eyes. Her long legs gave her a statuesque beauty that guaranteed her attention in any crowd.

The good priest was also watching as she disappeared into the sultry night. A worried frown settled over his face, though he told himself there was little reason for concern. Sigourney Hamilton was adept at obtaining sharply honed political interviews with world leaders, interviews that were seldom flattering. The year before she had received the St. Vincent Prize, the Italian equivalent of the Pulitzer Prize, for her incisive and penetrating series on Libya's infamous Khadafi.

Knowing Sigourney and her drive to succeed in order to overcome her rude beginnings, she was after the Pulitzer now. However, she was coming to Constantine at a time when the political atmosphere was highly charged.

Macedonia was about to celebrate the week of Midsummer Midnight in honor of the glorious Twentieth of July, when the Macedonians had revolted against the tyrannical Turkish rule in 1825. Father Murphy was all too aware of the dangerous unrest that roiled beneath Macedonia's festive atmosphere. He was an integral part of that unrest.

The taxi shot into the swirling blur of Constantine traffic. Sigourney noticed that one or two armed soldiers were posted at almost every corner, as common as gasoline stations in Los Angeles. Only in terms of population was Constantine a similar metropolis, though. In 1825, three hundred houses had clustered around the sacred hill of the capital's acropolis, a citadel with fifteen-foot-thick walls. Now the spreading bulk of the city took in one hundred fifty-five square miles filled by nearly two million people.

Sagging with jet lag, Sigourney rested her head against the back of the seat. Street lights flashing by illuminated the taxi's bizarre interior in a strobe effect. Some kind of lacy material curtained the back windows, and a vase of flowers was anchored to the dash. Below it, a cassette player blared a folk song.

At a circular intersection the driver all but ignored the policeman in his pulpit, who was directing traffic with the mannered grace of a ballet dancer. When the taxi dodged violently into another lane and shot forward at an even faster pace, Sigourney's head jerked upright and her hand grabbed for the armrest.

As the driver adroitly dodged trolley buses, carts and pedestrians, she relaxed a bit—until he roared down the wrong side of the boulevard. She froze when a donkey hauling a wagon plodded leisurely in front of the hurtling cab. A cyclist with a bundle of firewood, followed by a single file of sheep, started into the intersection from the other side. The taxi's horn shrieked its dismay. The driver swerved off the main thoroughfare that led eventually into Old Town and instead bumped down a narrow dirt road and braked to a whiplash-inducing halt.

"My God!" she cried. "This is worse than Tokyo!"

She couldn't follow the old man's rapid burst of Greek, but his frightened gestures were not encouraging, especially when first his door, then the one closest to her, were flung open. A large hand smothered her scream.

"Neither you nor the old man will be hurt," a low, rich baritone voice reassured her in English. It was a voice one never could forget.

In front of her the old man was pulled from behind the wheel, and another man, only a shadow in the darkness, took his place. Terrified, she lunged for the door opposite her. Her breath was forced from her lungs by her abductor's solid weight. Pinned flat on the spring-punctured seat, she lay still, feeling his warm breath against her cheek.

"I am with the Pan-Hellenic Free Forces. I want only to talk with you. Will you cooperate?"

Hysterical laughter bubbled in her throat. In the sudden blackness of the isolated lane the man seemed capable of the most extreme mayhem. She managed a nod of her head.

He sat up, releasing her, and she breathed again. She tried to make out the passenger's features, but the curtained darkness of the lonely, tree-lined street was a little unnerving, and she tasted the metallic beginnings of real fear on her tongue.

Rapidly she tried to remember what she knew about the Pan-Hellenic Free Forces. She recalled vaguely that the Pan-Hellenic movement was some kind of an underground segment of Agamemnon's legal political opposition, the New Democracy Party. She also remembered reading somewhere that the PFF disclaimed links to the outlawed Macedonian Provisional Army—terrorists—but espoused the MPA's cause: a democratic constitution and the abolition of the military regime, which had turned Macedonia into a police state.

The engine purred back to life, and the new driver shot the taxi forward down the rutted road.

"In the series of interviews you are doing on Agamemnon," the man at her side said, "I want you to include the position of the Pan-Hellenic Free Forces."

"How did you know I was here to—"

He cut her off. "I have no time for explanations. The world must understand that the Pan-Hellenic Free Forces is not a terrorist organization but rather one of defense and restraint. We disapprove of the terror tactics of the Macedonian Provisional Army. But if the United Nations continues to turn a blind eye while Agamemnon's military and secret police oppress us, we will not limit ourselves to defense only."

She was intrigued by his resonant baritone, by both the gentleness and the bitterness inflected in his speech. "Who are you?" she asked, wanting him to continue so she could hear more of his marvelous voice, and unaware that her interest in him was overcoming her initial fear.

"My name is not necessary, Miss Hamilton. What is necessary is that the world must know the truth about the suppression of freedom here in what was once the cradle of democracy. The roots of the entire Western world's system of government and politics and religion were in this corner of the Aegean."

There was a sense of controlled urgency as he talked, shifting in the seat to address her. His voice was made even more terse by the force of his convictions. She wished she could see his features better. From the give of the taxi's seat—and the memory of his solid weight—she could tell he was a big man, and she felt a second stab of fear—not of harm, really, but a woman's innate fear of territorial invasion by any male.

"This military regime," he continued, "is committed to annihilating any political opposition—but specifically the New Democracy Party—to totally abolishing all civil rights and even outlawing religious practices."

In the confinement of the back seat her exhausted body felt the power of his anger like an invigorating breeze.

"Isn't the United Nations supposed to be keeping order in Macedonia?"

"General Agamemnon's bombing of the St. Paul Greek Orthodox Church last week proves their ineffectiveness," he snapped.

"*New Report* attributed the bombing to Russian-trained guerrillas," she said with a dismissive sweep of her hand. "The general was quoted as indicating that certain foreign powers were trying to provoke a confrontation between the church and the state."

"That is because Agamemnon does not want the UN and the rest of the world to know that it was the work of his secret police," he said. "Or that the suppressed people of Macedonia are staging a revolution against his dictatorship."

"Grammarians would hasten to make the point that a revolution is a revolution only if it succeeds," she said. "Otherwise it is a rebellion."

His laugh was cynical. "Ahh, yes—I forget I am talking to a specialist in semantics," he said, and she could detect the taunt in his voice. "Let *me* quote *News Report*. 'Each interview is a portrait of myself. The interviews are a strange mixture of my ideas, my temperament, my patience, all of them driving the questions....An interview is a love story for me.' Or something to that effect, am I not right?"

They were her words all right, yet the way he said them, his intonation and inflection, colored their meaning, as she knew he had meant to do. Unable to help herself, she blushed right down to the neat neckline of her dress.

"Then you know," she said, "that the article later quotes me as saying I really get interested in my subjects. I get in fights and discussions, and I yell and scream and—"

"Checkpoint!" the driver cried out.

The taxi slowed as it neared the barricade. The harsh glare from a spotlight alongside the barrier spilled into the interior of the taxi. Its light revealed her companion at last. His lean and lined profile suggested a man of some experience, maybe forty or so. There was something gorgeous about him—and slightly dangerous, too. A flash of violence, controlled but powerful, a quick turn toward her and a look that said, "Just be careful." Yet, somehow, she knew he meant her no harm.

With what was for her a rare bit of feminine vanity, she wondered what he thought of her. Did he find her beautiful?

"If they ask, we're newlyweds on our honeymoon," he ordered. Then he surprised her by taking her hands and drawing them around his massive, barrelled rib cage. With a shock she felt the knife sheathed under his left arm. The second shock came when he bent his head and kissed her.

Stunned, she returned the kiss, half out of response to his authoritative control of the situation and half from curiosity—and not a little excitement. She had always asserted that those who became blasé did so because they had no imagination and no sense of risk taking.

Though his fingers gently cupped her face, his mouth and his kiss consumed her. His lips moving over hers were like electrical charges. In her thirty-seven years she had been kissed by a score or more of men—of all nationalities and occupations—from an Oriental prime minister to a Brazilian movie star to an out-of-work Brooklyn bricklayer.

About those passing romantic encounters—she had felt what? Blasé, after all? Certainly she considered herself an informed, sophisticated woman who harbored no misconceptions about the mystery of sexual attraction. In truth, she had felt a certain vague dissatisfaction.

Yet now all of her arrogant assurance—the certainty that she was too intelligent to delude herself with an affair merely to escape the boredom of one's self—was being melted into oblivion by the mastery of this political outlaw's deep kiss.

At last he released her, raising his head, but still cupping her face with calloused hands, when a voice ordered curtly in English, "All right, out of the car." She knew then that it was a UN roadblock.

"Slide out on your side," her newly acquired husband whispered. "And avoid any quick gestures that might be taken as threats."

She did as he instructed, while he got out the far side. The driver, a young man with peach fuzz still on his face, was nervously presenting his papers to one of the three soldiers who manned the spotlit barrier. One wore American army fatigues with a UN armband; the other two were dressed in the olive khaki of the gendarmerie,

Macedonia's paramilitary force. All three cradled automatic weapons in the crooks of their arms.

"Your identification papers," one of the gendarmes demanded in Macedonia's dialect of the modern Greek language.

Her own Greek was rusty from years of little use, and when she did not respond immediately the soldier lifted the muzzle of his gun toward her midsection. A false move and she might be cut in half. The whole incident was playing like a bad B movie. Nonetheless, she realized that she was in a country where people were summarily arrested, tortured, even executed, by the VASIK, an acronym of Agamemnon's Gestapo-like secret police. Mechanically she withdrew her passport from her purse and passed it to the soldier.

With an appreciative glance at her face, he began to flip through the stamped pages.

"What do you think you are doing?" demanded the man who had just kissed her, striding to her side to curl a powerful and possessive arm about her waist.

The gendarme glared menacingly at him, but her companion yanked her passport from the soldier's hands and waved it before the man's face.

"*Vlacho!* Peasant! You have it upside down, you big ape. See! It's an American passport. American! Look— see this? This is her press card. Do you realize the power of the press against *vlachos* like you?"

When he shoved the muzzle of the gendarme's gun aside, the soldier's finger slid onto the trigger, but the big man at her side continued to rage. "My bride and I are spending tomorrow with General Agamemnon, and I mean for him to know how shoddily you treat visitors. Important official American visitors!''

The invocation of Agamemnon's name was like an open sesame. The soldiers shot sidelong glances at one another. The American lowered his M-16 and nodded at the gendarmes. ''These papers look okay to me. You can pass.''

The driver acted as though he couldn't get back in the car quickly enough. Sigourney slid into the rear seat next to the outlaw, who took her hand in his big one in what appeared to be a loving gesture. After one of the gendarmes waved them on, she slumped back, her head nestled against the indentation formed by the man's bicep and the steel plate that was his chest muscle. Her stomach was lurching toward her throat.

''Just take several slow, deep breaths,'' he said. ''You did well.''

The shaking of her hands infected the rest of her limbs, and she began to shiver uncontrollably. He wrapped his other arm around her and hugged her firmly yet tenderly. ''It is over now.''

''No,'' she managed. ''It's never over for me. You see, I'm a coward through and through. I'm a champion when it comes to running for shelter. What you see is sheer bravado.'' She sat up, pulling gently away from his embrace. A sensual vise, his grasp shook her more, perhaps, than the close call at the roadblock had.

''Courage does not necessarily imply a lack of fear.''

''I'm all right now. Do you have a cigarette?''

He drew a pack from his shirt pocket and shook one out. "They're Turkish and rather strong."

She tilted her head to the lighter he offered, and in the flare of its light saw more clearly the planes of his face. A little wary, a little haunted, his face was a gorgeous battlefield that appeared to be distilled from his very essence. She dragged deeply on the pungent smoke and looked away from the impaling, dark-eyed gaze.

"I'm afraid I can't use your statement in my article," she said to stay a feeling of impending peril that had begun to build when she had first gotten into the cab. "I portray people in my interviews, not ideals. Give your statement to UP or API or, for that matter, *News Report*."

"Then you write only for sensationalism," he said, impatience and something else, perhaps disgust, edging his voice.

"Listen, if I'm a painter and I do a portrait, have I or haven't I the right to paint the subject as I choose?"

He leaned forward and tapped the driver's shoulder, then turned to her. "Thank you for your valuable time, Miss Hamilton," he said. The car braked, and he slipped back into the darkness without another word or gesture.

From the balcony of her hotel room high above the city, Sigourney watched bonfires flare like matches against the black night sky. They would burn until dawn. To the north, near the acropolis, was Old Town, where motor traffic was banned and where crusading knights had once clanked about in their armor. To the west, near the marketplace, was the famed Melos Temple, with its marble lions and colossal statue of Bacchus. Farther on was the Parthenon-columned Royal Palace, now the offices of the Macedonian premier and his sinister cabinet.

She wrapped the *déshabillé* of ivory silk more tightly about her body, although the night was warm with the summer solstice. She remembered another night very like this one. From a carefree and giddy cocktail party on the roof garden of the Caravelle Hotel, she had watched a rocket attack on Saigon. That had been one of her first assignments. Since then, she had covered the political and social upheavals on five continents.

Before Saigon, there had been the superficiality of interviews with celebrities—entertainers, novelists, royalty. Their *antipatici*, the sullen boredom of the jet set, had almost suffocated her.

Rather than try to explain the bloodthirsty madness of battle, as war correspondents were driven to do—and she had never read any column that offered any satisfactory explanation—she chose instead to write about the leaders who sent young men to war. Early on she had observed that world leaders always kept themselves at a safe distance from actual gunfire, and that was exactly where she herself preferred to be.

She had even come to terms with the terror of her own childhood, but it wasn't something on which she let herself dwell. Her thoughts skipped to the mysterious man she had met a short time before. The sweet/strong taste of his Turkish cigarette lingered in her mouth. As did the memory of his kiss on her lips.

What did she know about him? Not even his name. Some reporter she was. She couldn't decide what was disturbing her, except that his presence had left a strong imprint. She was naturally suspicious of his male beauty. Then, too, she was philosophically unsympathetic to his ideals.

She had sat across the table from many of the world's leaders, but this political renegade was more impressive than any mogul she had ever met. He possessed a keen vitality that was passionately tangible.

No longer was she ready for bed, rather she felt disjangled and at odds with herself, filled with a twitching restlessness that inoculated her against the sleep she had so craved earlier.

Chapter 2

The jade sheath of raw silk, playing against the golden expanse of Sigourney's skin, created a sensational, dramatic effect, exactly what she sought for the audience with his eminence, General Agamemnon. As she strode into his cavernous office, she noted Agamemnon's atavistic baring of the teeth in what was supposed to pass for a smile.

Georgios Agamemnon fitted the pattern she had discerned early on in certain kinds of political leaders, usually those who had quickly promoted themselves from foot soldier to army commander to executive leader with absolute power. Though not necessarily intelligent, these people were foxlike in their dealings with the international community. They had an uncanny sense of the theatrical and of timing; they were egotists who frequently bordered on megalomania. And they all had one outstanding characteristic in common: They were usually not physically prepossessing, Napoleon and Hitler being two extreme examples.

General Agamemnon was a third.

Short and slight, with dark, wiry hair and a florid complexion, he faced her across the broad expanse of his cypress desk. A multiplicity of medals spangled his uniform. The "smile" stretched the thin slit of his mouth, but something glacial sieved through.

Behind him, at either side of French doors, stood the blue and white Macedonian flag and the silver flag of the Chief of State, his personal insignia. Outside the doors were two white-kilted, red-capped *evzones* of the Royal Guard armed with Uzi machine pistols. Beyond the colorful sentries were garden pools and pebbled paths and spectacular grounds belying a deadly menace as palpable as the serpent in Eden.

Behind Sigourney was an enormous gilt-framed, beveled mirror, a gift of the Republic of Kenya. Below it, on a damask chair in the corner, lurked the dome-plated Colonel Anatolia Kopeta, head of the dreaded VASIK security police. He reminded her of a Sumo wrestler or, better, she thought, a malevolent toad. In a way, Colonel Kopeta was more dangerous than Agamemnon. Within VASIK's covert world, Kopeta moved discreetly and lethally.

He had emigrated to the United States in 1941 when the Nazis had invaded Greece. His experience as a policeman for the Macedonian prewar royal government had been put to quick use by the Ivy League operators who later called themselves the Office of Strategic Services. The OSS sent Anatolia Kopeta back to Europe to supervise a number of agents in neighboring Yugoslavia. After the war and the Greek communist takeover effort in 1948, he went underground and branched out on his own. Why was he present at the interview?

For the moment she tucked the question away. She had looked forward to this series of meetings with Agamemnon, knowing that it could mean the Pulitzer Prize she coveted. She was ready to begin.

Depending on the preference of her subject, she conducted her interviews in Italian, French, Spanish, or English. Agamemnon preferred English. Though she alternately cajoled, badgered and charmed her subjects, for those like Agamemnon she invariably began each session with a provocative question.

She had been shown to a short-legged chair in front of the desk; now she perched on the edge of its seat and, leaning forward, said with a disarming smile, "You're not a pacificist, are you? To what extent does power fascinate you? Try to be sincere."

His smile frozen, Agamemnon settled against the throne-sized leather swivel chair with a quick glance at Kopeta. "Only to the extent it helps my country and my people."

A thought flashed into her mind of the man she had met the night before, a leader of the resistance, and his similar claim for concern for his country and his people, so typical of all "leaders."

"Certain elements within your own country would disagree," she replied. "They would say that you are a bloodthirsty dictator."

The general hunched forward, his jaw jutting. "I take offense at such a statement. You must remember that the coup that sent King Philip into exile and thrust me into power was relatively bloodless."

"True, for a few weeks. But since then, General, it has been charged that your regime has been marked by blood and violence."

In the background Colonel Kopeta remained ominously quiet. Agamemnon shrugged rounded shoulders topped by ornate epaulets. "Political scientists classify these killings as the usual purge that occurs after a change in power. It happened with your American Revolution. American and British specialists in Euro-Mideast affairs believe things will settle down as soon as our government is stabilized."

"I would think eleven years of rule should have stabilized the government by now."

"But it has. I have launched the biggest construction project in Macedonia's history with the establishment of our international shipyards." His obsidian eyes glittered with his eagerness to inform the world press of his accomplishments. "As a goodwill gesture in celebration of Midsummer Midnight Week, I released two detained Britons only a few hours ago. For the first time in Macedonia, medicine and education are free."

"It would seem you've transformed Macedonia into a socialist state."

Keeping her subject off-balance was a tactic she had often successfully employed. Abruptly she switched the interview to another direction. "Your centuries-old mansion in the Thessalonian foothills is considered one of the supreme works of Macedonian architecture and is elegantly furnished, I understand."

Agamemnon's face brightened. "You must see it to appreciate its full beauty. I will arrange for—"

"Rather ostentatious for someone who espouses the Spartan life, isn't it, General?"

Before he could manage a reply, she rose and snapped off her tape recorder. She would let him stew about that for a while. "I'll continue with the interview later. Perhaps next week, if I may. And I'm sure I'll see you at the Midsummer Midnight gala tonight. Here at the Royal Palace, isn't it?"

The venerable taverna in Old Town indulged the Macedonian taste for dining alfresco. With siesta over, the brightly painted chairs in the sidewalk cafe were filled with chattering customers.

Sigourney found Father Murphy at a table next to a pitted pastel wall. A fragrant, white-blossomed locust tree shaded the table from the hot afternoon sun and cast the priest's companion in shadows. Even when the man rose from the shadows to pull out a chair for her, she didn't immediately recognize him—until he said, "Good afternoon, Miss Hamilton," in the marvelously textured voice from the night before.

Sliding into the chair, she steeled herself to reply calmly. "Good afternoon." She directed an accusing glance at the hulking old priest. "I take it you're part of this conspiracy?"

Father Murphy folded his gnarled hands, looked skyward as if for a spiritual intervention and, when none appeared forthcoming, sighed. "As of this morning, I'm afraid so. When I learned that Damon here had approached you last night, I agreed to introduce you more formally."

So Damon was his name. Damon, Greek for the Constant One. She sensed that in whatever he did he would be constant, committed, thorough. Damon—what?

"I confess to being guilty as charged," Father Murphy continued. "Aiding and abetting, the Vatican would call it. Accomplice before the fact. My calling will be in ruins. My reputation will be...well, my *calling* anyway will be damaged by the discovery that I have compromised my moral rectitude by arranging a tryst."

"Whatever this holy man confesses, Miss Hamilton, it is I and I alone who am responsible."

At last Sigourney let herself meet Damon's gaze. She could not deny the chemistry she felt in his presence. He measured her while she inspected him. The neck, as thickly muscled as a linebacker's, was tieless, but a tweed jacket somewhat civilized the man. Did he wear it to cover the knife sheathed beneath his armpit?

With wildly curling blond hair and blue eyes that were almost black in the hard, handsome face, this tawny Adonis across from her doubtlessly resembled, she surmised, the historic Macedonian leader, Alexander the Great. "You're taking a chance, aren't you—appearing in public in broad daylight?"

A white-aproned waiter approached to take their order for Turkish coffee; then Damon fastened his attention on her, though she sensed that he had not completely released her from his regard even during that brief interruption. "I do not always skulk around by the dark of the moon."

So, he could smile, even if his eyes didn't. They were like dark, sapphire marbles: opaque. Determining what was going on behind them was impossible.

"Besides," he said, "I have found that acting in a natural manner, doing exactly what the opposition would least expect, is the best protection."

He offered her a cigarette, but she smiled easily and shook her head. "I just bought a pack at a kiosk down the street." She broadened her smile. "An American brand."

After inhaling, he said. "Tell me, Miss Hamilton, why are you not writing articles about women for one of the fashionable magazines?" Rather than holding the cigarette between his fingers, he held it with his thumb and forefinger, so his palm shielded its burning end. "After all, women are a much more timely subject, no?"

The question was bland enough, yet she found herself replying defensively, perhaps because she wasn't certain she even liked him.

"I try to avoid writing about women or about problems concerning women. Women are not a special breed, and I don't see why they should be treated as a separate subject, like sports or the weather."

"But you treat women in marriage as a special subject. 'Marriage is not a word, it is a sentence.'"

She took several pistachios from the earthen bowl in the center of the table and said evenly, "You have a remarkable, amazing memory, Mr.—?"

"Demetrios. A rather feminist view on marriage, isn't it?"

After the waiter had brought their coffee, thick and sweetly pungent in small thin cups, Father Murphy sought to ease the strained conversation. "Truth is, Damon, once Sigourney beheld my virile features, unimpaired by conventional regularity, she found she could give her heart in marriage to no other man."

Sigourney laughed lightly. "That's why you became a priest, isn't it, Father? To escape my clutches."

"Father Murphy has told me only that you have been friends for some years," Damon said. "How did you meet?"

"Shall I reveal all the lascivious details, my child, or shall we let you remain a lady of mystery?"

She shrugged and sipped the coffee. It tasted like bitter molasses and was almost as thick. "You might say that this disreputable man here—actually he was a man of God, even then—took me off the streets of Seoul. I was a war orphan, and he arranged for me to be adopted by an American couple, the Hamiltons. That was—what, Father? Nearly thirty years ago?"

The priest pumped his grizzled brows up and down. "Please, Sigourney, alluding to so many years is demeaning to a virile man of my age."

A mustachioed old man playing an accordion strolled near their table. Abruptly, Damon ground out his cigarette and leaned forward. "Miss Hamilton, I want you to reconsider my proposal. In fact, more than including just a statement in your article, I want you to do an entire series on the atrocities being committed in the name of government in Macedonia. Father Murphy will answer whatever questions you might have."

With that, Damon rose and vanished in the bustle of afternoon strollers. Sigourney picked up her coffee cup. "A congenial fellow."

"You might say circumstances forced his sudden departure." He popped a pistachio into his cavernous, yellow-toothed mouth. "Damon's strong feelings for the PFF tend to make him a trifle uncivilized at times."

"Surely you exaggerate," she said dryly. "Tell me about this man of inimitable charm."

"I thought you wanted to know about the PFF."

"Did I say that?"

The priest's shoulders bumped up expressively. "Alas, I am losing my appeal. I knew it would happen sooner or later, but…but how sad that it is Damon Demetrios you want to know about and not me.

"Well, what can I tell you? I could tell you about his parents—that they are farmers—and that he has a younger sister, but I have a suspicion that you are really more interested in him than his family."

"You're baiting me, Father Murphy."

The slack mouth quivered with good humor, then sobered into a straight line. "I will tell you that Demetrios disdains politicians. He is really an apolitical animal. To him, politics is nothing but a big, losing game, where the citizen is ripped off."

"I would like to hear more of the personal aspects of Damon Demetrios."

"I was afraid of that." He sighed. "All right. Damon hates silly questions. He is standoffish, aloof, reflective, unyielding and distant."

"So far you haven't told me anything I hadn't already perceived," she chided.

"I understand that besides Greek and English, he has mastered German, Russian and French."

"Go on."

"I take it you want me to be more specific. Then I shall. He cannot stand for people to try to get too close to him. That comes, perhaps, from having survived two years in solitary confinement in Toridallos Military Prison, which is where I met him when I was ministering to the political prisoners."

Toridallos Prison. She had heard of the place; it had the reputation as one of the worst anywhere in the world.

"I *will* tell you that Damon's elusiveness is the key to his sexual charisma. And that he was married. Anything else of a personal nature, Sigourney, you should ask him." He paused. "Except—don't get emotionally involved with him, my child." He put his hand over hers.

"This is really unlike you, you know. You were never one for romantic flings."

With a smile she drew her hand away and, retrieving her purse, stood up. "You truly are maligning me, Father. My journalist's curiosity was merely asserting itself. Give me a call tomorrow. If you can arrange time out from your illegal activities, maybe you can show me some of Macedonia's reputed grandeur."

Diamonds were as common as worry beads at the Royal Palace that night. Several string quartets in tuxedos moved about the enormous marbled rooms playing classical music and folk tunes of Macedonia, like the quick, staccato *tsamiko*.

In the main salon, embellished with huge baroque crystal chandeliers, heavy silk drapes and thickly tufted satin couches, servants in red and gold livery served Dom Perignon in delicate flutes and mounds of Caspian caviar, or hovered expectantly but discreetly.

Luminaries of the political world, along with international tycoons and royalty from other nations, soaked up the glitter of the evening. Also circulating through the hubbub were the wealthy of Macedonia, who had continued to consolidate and exploit their positions during Agamemnon's reign.

Photographers fluttered about feverishly, imploring the beautiful people to clear a path for their shots, and swirls of strobe flashes collided in the opulent hall.

Celebrity coverage was definitely not one of Sigourney's interests. She knew a handful of the hundred or so guests by sight, from charity balls in Monte Carlo, art openings in London, or from one of the avant-garde tanning grounds like St. Tropez or the Côte d'Azur. If she wanted, she could mingle among the guests effortlessly; her adoptive American parents, successful entrepreneurs in the finest tradition, had seen to it that she received the best education, including a two-year stint at a prestigious boarding school outside Lausanne and three summers at the Sorbonne in Paris.

Though no one would ever have guessed, she was basically shy. All the patina so carefully applied by her adoptive parents could not erase those first seven years of blight. Hobnobbing with the elite was something she would leave to the status seekers and the nouveau riche.

As usual, she could have passed for royalty that evening. Her thick hair was sleeked back into an intricate French knot. A rope of cultivated pearls served as the line of demarcation between the flawless beauty of her skin and the floor-length black Halston whose bias-cut chiffon clung to her gently curved hips and wafted magnetically behind her.

With an elbow-length white glove dangling from one hand and a crystal goblet of rare Tuscany wine grasped lightly in the other, she moved like a spirit among the other guests, her sharp mind snapping mental pictures to be played back in her hotel room later that night.

A balding attaché attached himself to her. Laving her with a fine spray of spittle, he extemporized on olives. "Excuse me," she said abruptly, and strode away without a word of explanation.

The Macedonian Salon was a dining room of immense proportions with a tapestried backdrop for crimson-clothed tables set with English bone china and gold-rimmed crystal. She estimated that the general must have laid out at least fifteen thousand dollars for the evening.

Her name card placed her at a table with Alexos Oristos, a shipping magnate who controlled most of the world's privately owned oil tankers. A short, stocky man with iron gray hair, he fancied himself a Lothario, having been married both to an Italian opera coloratura and the widow of a ranking American politician.

She suffered through his flirtations and picked at her meal. Fortunately, a verbose blue-haired matron claimed his attention through the rest of dinner. The liver-spotted ancient on Sigourney's other side made an attempt at conversation, but when she replied that she was a writer and offered no credentials, he looked at her sympathetically and lost interest.

At his table General Agamemnon conversed with the Duchess of Lombardy, his hands waving expansively as he lectured. When he spotted Sigourney, he flashed her a patronizing smile, which she pretended not to notice. With a start, she realized she was bored.

Unwilling to let boredom dictate her life, even for the sake of an interview, she would normally have called it an evening early, but after dinner her escape was cut short when Oristos cornered her and maneuvered her into the ballroom for a dance. She was on the verge of being rude, but stifled her impatience. After all, he was a source of information; she could use what he told her in her series in Agamemnon.

As they waltzed—and for all his girth Oristos was an expert dancer—she smiled politely and said in Italian, "You Hellenics have been seafarers since almost the beginning of civilization, I understand."

"We are descendants of roaming voyagers," he replied in the same language, as his hand did its own roaming along her spine. "The Odyssey, the Iliad, Jason and the Argonauts," he continued, his breath hot and garlicky on her face, "they all point up our seafaring heritage."

"Your shipping ventures have flourished quite profitably under Agamemnon's regime, haven't they?"

Abruptly Oristos's hand ceased its wandering. "No more than they did under King Philip," he replied, this time in Greek.

He seemed almost relieved when someone cut in on them, and he relinquished her with elaborate gallantry. Looking up with a start, she recognized her new partner: Damon Demetrios again. He was very handsome in the formal attire. Very civilized looking, though she suspected that in reality he was anything but. His eyes warned her that the underground world he inhabited was full of danger and terror.

Wordlessly, she slipped into his arms. Where was her whipcord tongue now, the stiletto repartee she had developed to conceal her shyness?

His touch, firm at the small of her back, burned through the chiffon. After a moment she allowed herself to look up into his handsome face. A tabula rasa. "I understand this affair was by invitation only," she murmured. "A highly restricted guest list."

His glance barely flicked over her face. As they turned to the music his eyes scanned the ballroom in a steady, continuous arc. What was going on behind those eyes? Was he an intelligent, concerned human being, or merely an obedient automaton in that antidictatorship organization?

"I presented my invitation to the doorman." His gaze drifted momentarily to hers. "Unfortunately, there is a couple somewhere in Constantine tonight who are frantically searching for their misplaced envelope."

Beneath the sweep of her high Oriental cheekbones, dimples formed in a spontaneous smile. "I admire your daring and courage."

His eyes were coldly speculative. "Enough to spend a couple of days with me?"

His question silenced her, and he continued. "Father Murphy told me that you were uninterested in the dry facts concerning the Pan-Hellenic Free Forces."

Had Father Murphy told him in just what subject she *was* interested? "Did he?" she asked, insouciance overlaying her carefully selected reply.

"Since you mentioned to him this afternoon that you would like to see some of the Macedonian countryside, I thought I would act as your guide."

"You want to convince me of the necessity of your covert organization?" she asked flatly.

"Ultimately, yes."

She should have guessed that was what he wanted from her. She felt young, and very foolish, hot and cold at once. He was offering himself as an interview subject in place of the PFF, as a sacrifice. It galled her.

"Did you risk your life to come here only for that reason?"

"Hardly. My life is too important to the PFF for such a irresponsible, negligent act." His voice, that low, rich rumble, contained nothing of flamboyance or bravado. Only a statement. "If I wanted to convince you, I would choose a less risky way."

"Such as?"

"Such as waiting for you in your hotel room tonight. But the gala offered additional possibilities—scouting the number and positions of the royal guards, looking for the most approachable of Agamemnon's aristocratic lackeys, the identification of any recent additions to his secret police."

Indignation stirred in her. "You seem to have read enough about me to—"

"I have a full dossier."

The knowledge shook her for a moment. "—to know that there are many people who have attempted to utilize through me the power of the press. They've resorted to everything from flattery to bribery, and none has succeeded. I choose whom I want for my subjects."

"Your unvarnished opinion is highly regarded."

She stiffened in his embrace. "I wasn't angling for a compliment. I know my own worth without having to ask others to confirm it."

"For such a radical, Miss Hamilton, you live rather extravagantly—a twenty-three-room mansion in Carmel, California, and a modest million-dollar brownstone in Washington."

She shrugged, though inside she didn't feel so indifferent. "I've earned everything I own. Journalism is a terrible privilege. I don't exaggerate when I say that in every interview I leave some of my soul."

"And integrity? Are you willing to see both sides of an issue?"

"I've never been accused of being narrow-minded, Mr.—"

His sudden dark warning glance cut her short. "Then meet me tomorrow morning out on the old Istanbul road. A taxi will be waiting for you outside your hotel at ten."

"I don't know—"

The waltz ended, and he released her. Lifting the tips of her fingers to his lips in the timeless gesture of Old World etiquette, he deserted her and disappeared in the mass of guests.

In the darkness, Sigourney sat in her hotel room's overstuffed chair and puffed on a cigarette while deciding that she would reason out the issue logically.

Honesty made her admit that she wanted to see the big Macedonian again because—if for no other reason—she would be disturbed until she did. However, the instinctive self-preservation that had guided her as a child through the madness of the Korean war alerted her to the danger she was courting.

She asked herself again what she knew about him. Certainly she had never met another man exactly like him. There was a menacing potential in his dark quietness and his tremendous power. She crossed to the balcony doors and tossed her half-smoked cigarette over the white wrought-iron railing. Their encounter that night was still so recent, so strong, so disturbing, that she could not put him from her mind.

Damon Demetrios was a man who made you come to him. He held his ground, and either you entered his turf or you didn't get him, period. He would not court a woman.

He had been married, Father Murphy had said. Had Damon courted his wife? Had he loved her?

She returned to the chair. What was it that Father Murphy had said about Damon—that his elusiveness was the key to his sexual charisma?

He was extraordinary, this freedom fighter. But she didn't enjoy the prospect of being drawn against her will into his eerie and perilous world.

She recalled the sensation she had felt in his arms as they danced. Again she saw those penetrating eyes that read her mind so mockingly.

Suddenly she stood and began to pace the room. She felt as if she had St. Vitus's dance. Sitting, rising, sitting, standing, walking.

She was certain now that behind those unfathomable eyes was layer upon layer of complex emotional matter.

What plots, what tricks, ran through his brain? Was he ever frightened? Could he even experience fear?

She grabbed her beaded purse from the nightstand and riffled through it for another cigarette. After a soothing puff she was able to reassure herself that she was not mystically drawn to this man. She had merely been jolted by infatuation, but it was an infatuation stronger than any she had ever known.

Chapter 3

A red Fiat was parked under the wind-twisted branches of a dusty olive tree. Sigourney felt the quickening of her pulse at the sight of the little car.

The taxi driver, the same young man who had evicted her driver from the airport, glanced nervously in his rearview mirror at the serpentine road dwindling behind them, then pulled the taxi alongside the Fiat. The man in the driver's seat wore mirrored sunglasses, but she could easily recognize him.

Sigourney left the taxi and, stashing her small carry-on behind the Fiat's passenger's seat, slid in next to him. The car was compact and their thighs almost touched. Damon was so big that he nearly filled the whole front seat—yet there wasn't an ounce of excess flesh on him.

He was all hard muscle and bone and corpuscles that were surely composed of liquid steel.

"You knew I'd come?" she asked.

He smiled, and she thought how very pleasant his smile could be, and how white was the flash of his strong teeth. His jaw was like smooth brick. "I am pleased that you did, Miss Hamilton."

This man had kissed her as no other man had, yet he still addressed her formally. "You didn't answer my question. You knew I'd come, didn't you?"

He wheeled the car back onto the road. "You would not be the excellent journalist you are if you had not."

As the taxi driver had, he glanced carefully in the rearview mirror, and she asked, "Are you worried about our being followed?"

"Both the taxi and the Fiat are rented and would be difficult to trace, but I would not put it past Agamemnon's henchmen to pick up your trail."

Recalling the hulking Kopeta, she mentally shivered. "That explains the labyrinth of backstreets the taxi took, but why would they follow *me*?"

"You are a foreigner—and a world-renowned reporter. That makes you immediately suspect. The fact that you delayed your series of interviews with Agamemnon until next week assured of drawing a tail."

Uneasily, she glanced behind her, saying, "How did you know I delayed the interviews?"

"We have our own sources. By the way, you have heard of the Colossus of Rhodes? I thought we'd start your tour there, with the Aegean Islands first."

She wished he would remove the sunglasses, but it wouldn't really make a difference. The eyes were just as mirrorlike. "I thought Rhodes—and the sea—were to the south of Constantine. Aren't we going east?"

Beneath the glasses, Damon's mobile lips curled into a wry grin. "Owing to my uncommon occupation, we cannot pass through the usual customs points when we leave the mainland. So we will use an old smugglers' cove."

She laughed. "I think I'm about to embark on one of those extraordinary tours the travel agencies always promise and never come through with."

The narrow road climbed and wound through fields spangled with wildflowers as it linked village to village. In breathtaking fashion it sometimes skirted sheer cliffs. Pleasant valleys, their hillsides terraced to the last foot, supported wheat fields and orange groves, where men and women scythed grass and cultivated their plots with heavy hoes.

With an unspoken temporary truce between them, Sigourney and Damon kept the conversation light, never mentioning the PFF.

When their conversation turned to reading, he said, "When I was a child, my family never trusted words much, and I guess I learned that physical movement was one of the best ways to express myself. But I did read newspapers and the occasional dog-eared paperback copies of the Greek classics that found their way to our mountain village."

"Greek classics? What happened to Classic Comics?"

"Of course, you would have read comic books as a child," he tossed back with a grin.

"Hardly. I was a voracious reader, but I didn't learn to read until after I came to live in the States, and I think I made up for lost time—Alexandre Dumas, Edgar Allan Poe, James Fenimore Cooper. Those novels were my escape from childhood unpleasantness. You know, I think I still look at the world as a child, with all the amazement and the rages of one."

"Which explains why your articles are so highly acclaimed. They have the candor, sometimes the rude forthrightness of a child, but without the innocence."

"If that's a compliment, thank you."

The conversation continued in an easy, relaxed vein, but she was always aware of him, of his potent masculinity. He pointed out an old herdsman entertaining his sheep with a reed pipe and, outside a village, women washing newly woven blankets in a stream. In a village of white-washed shuttered houses and bordering nosegays, he halted before a streetside grill.

"Our local fast-food stop," he said, and, unfolding his Goliath's body from the tiny car, went over to the aproned woman at the grill.

When he returned with a skewer of broiled lamb called *kokoretsi*, Sigourney said, "I refused to take my eyes off you. I was afraid you'd vanish as you have all three times I've been with you, and I certainly don't want to have to find my way back to Constantine alone."

"I will not desert you this week," he promised. The way he said it was the way of a man who chose his words carefully, a dedicated man who made no emotional commitments.

She was daintily licking the savory juices from her fingers when the road crested a ridge and presented them with an infinite expanse of rolling greenish-blue sea. The hot noon sun reflecting off the shimmering water almost blinded her. Below, a few yards out from the narrow stretch of white, sandy beach, a fishing boat with its sail furled bobbed like a cork in the swirl of the waves.

"Behold, your yacht awaits, mademoiselle."

She smiled, enjoying his easy humor, a quality she would not have believed existed in him. "You're a very resourceful man, Damon Demetrios."

At the base of the cliff stood a salty old man wearing a white billed cap, a dark blue shirt and sailor's trousers. When Damon got out of the car, he removed his sunglasses to clean them carefully with a handkerchief before pocketing them. As if that were a prearranged signal, the weathered man came forward and cast a curious but covert glance at Sigourney.

Damon handed him the Fiat's keys, saying, "Three days from now, eh, Naxos?"

The fisherman nodded. "Watch for the cutters patrolling off the coast, Damon."

After the old man drove away in the rented car, Damon surprised her by dropping to one knee before her. "Give me your foot, Sigourney."

It was the first time he had addressed her by her given name, and hearing it said in his deep, mellifluous voice stirred her, as did the touch of his hands around her left

ankle and instep as he removed her wedge-heeled sandal. Balanced on one foot, she put one hand on his muscled shoulder to steady herself. He was such a Samson
that even kneeling as he was, his tawny head cleared her
rib cage, and she was not considered short.

"Now," he said, when he had bared both her feet,
"spread your legs apart."

There was nothing seductive or insinuating in his voice;
still, she moved her feet warily into a spread-eagled
stance, feeling the sand warm and granular beneath her
bare feet.

He reached between her legs to grasp the rear hem of
her pink gingham skirt and drew it back through her legs
and up. "There," he said, tucking the hem into her
waistband and standing back to review the effect of the
dress hiked up her thighs in what was almost diaper
fashion. "You look the proper fishmonger's wife."

With a model's pirouette, she asked, "Is this supposed to be the latest in incognito attire?"

Damon's gaze moved past her and upward. She
turned, following its direction. On the bluff was a car,
and it wasn't the red Fiat. Two men, one wearing an orange sweatshirt and holding binoculars, stood next to the
car, watching them.

Damon waved one arm, the way one would in casual
acknowledgment to a stranger, or perhaps at a slight
acquaintance.

She shielded her eyes with her forearm the better to see
the two strangers. "You know them?"

"I would say it is a safe bet that they are Agamemnon's VASIK goons."

She squinted her eyes, trying to make out if either of the two was built like a Sumo wrestler, but, unexpectedly, Damon clasped her shoulders and drew her to him. His arms circled her back and her hips, molding her against his brawny length, and his mouth met hers with what might have been the simulation of a lover's kiss—or it might not have been. He did not give her a chance to ponder the issue.

When his tongue nudged insistently against her teeth, she opened her mouth. As his tongue explored the delicate insides of her mouth, she forgot her initial surprise, ignored the two watchers. The sound of the surf breaking, the feel of the salt-tanged breeze playing with her long hair, the strident cry of a gull overhead, all were obliterated in the exquisite, eternal moment of Damon's kiss.

Gradually she became aware of the sexual excitement building in her. She hated herself for responding so readily to him, even as her hands slipped up around the yard-wide shoulders and her lower torso swayed forward, pressing against his.

Damon's lips relinquished hers, but his mouth lingered against her cheek, his breath warm. Incredibly, she was shaken by this kiss even more than the first one in the back seat of the taxi. Off-balance emotionally, she tilted her head back, clinging to the steel-cable support of his upper arms. Dumbly, dazedly, she looked up into the dark blue eyes for some clue to his thoughts. Those once opaque eyes smoldered now. So, the statue could come to life after all.

"I liked that, Sigourney."

It was an awkward moment for her. She, who prized herself on her wit and frankness, could think of no appropriate response. To admit honestly that she liked it also might be construed as something much more. She had discovered early that her forthrightness, her lack of coyness, led men to the erroneous conclusion that she abided by the modern maxim: "If you desire a man, you sleep with him."

Instead, she evaded the issue, saying, "Agamemnon's goons are gone, but I doubt if you fooled them this time."

"Come on," he said, releasing her waist. Once more his voice held that normal social reserve common between strangers. "We need to wade out to the yawl while the tide is still with us."

Wanting to hide the hot blush of confusion that flagged her cheeks, she began to wade into the surf, while he removed his own shoes and rolled his pants legs above his heavily muscled calves.

By the time she gained the stern of the fishing boat, the crystalline water lapped up past her knees. But the cooling waves had no effect on the fire that licked inside her like a great solar flare.

Immediately behind her, Damon paused and tossed her carry-on and their shoes into the boat's bow; then his massive hands encircled her waist, overlapping easily in front and back, and he lifted her until she was sitting on the deck, her feet dangling over the side.

"Thank you," she told him, almost formally.

Damon boarded, and they were immediately on their way. He steered with a navigational instinct known by the Hellenes almost since time began. Overhead, the wind tugged at the mainmast to thrust the yawl toward the distant island of Rhodes. Occasionally she sighted a far-off speck of land that was a minor island.

The afternoon was one of those wine-colored days that could make her forget the double-barreled danger of Agamemnon's agents and Damon's passion. After a while she locked her hands about her knees and lazily turned her face upward, lids closed, to be kissed by the sun.

Sometime later, piqued with curiosity—and the overwhelming need to look at the man who disturbed her so—she slitted her lids, turning her gaze to the stern and Damon. The khaki shirt was open to his waist, revealing his chest, where the golden hair grew in whorls. Beneath the sunglasses he had once more donned, his mouth was grim and hard. From its set she knew his thoughts were not on her but on the two men who had seen them from the cliff.

How many women besides her had sensed in Damon that intensity, that devotion to a cause, and fled in relief? He was frightening, all right, but at the same time utterly intriguing. What would it be like to make love to the first man ever able to take her over completely? She trembled at the prospect. "Tell me more about Rhodes."

He focused his attention on her, his eyes piercing, and once more she experienced what it was to be wholly under his regard. The impact staggered her.

"Well, that particular island belongs to Greece. But there are hundreds of them fairly littering the Aegean Sea. I imagine that in a year or so Rhodes will become the newest récherché resort. Right now, though, only a few have discovered its secrets—countless churches, tombs, ancient and medieval treasures, sulphur baths still bubbling away, even a few modest villas tucked away in the hills."

"How did you discover all this?"

"When I was a little boy, our family used to make a pilgrimage every Easter to the Shrine of St. Paul. Tradition has it that the Apostle stopped at Rhodes in his itinerant preachings."

"I can't imagine you being a little boy."

He smiled. "I do not suppose I ever was. By the time I was thirteen I was already over six feet."

"And it looks like you haven't stopped growing yet. Is your father as tall as you?"

"He used to be, but age has stooped him a little. The people in our village will swear he had the strength of a lion."

She would wager that his son did, too.

"My father cut his teeth on an oxwhip. He was Old World, but he believed strongly in education; he even mastered English by reading a thumb-worn copy of the King James Bible that found its way to our village. He insisted that I leave there and go to live with an aunt and uncle in Constantine while I attended secondary school and then the university. That was my Uncle Naxos back at the cove."

"He looked just like the Cuban fisherman from *The Old Man and the Sea*."

"Appearances are deceiving, no? Now you tell me something about yourself."

"What can I say," she asked a little caustically, "that your organization hasn't already dug up?"

"You give away very little about your past—about your childhood."

She stared long and hard at Damon. The prospect of opening up to him was terribly tempting. But she knew that any liaison with him would endanger her carefully maintained barriers, threaten the security and the self-contentment that she had managed to achieve in life.

"I'm flattered by your interest," she said coolly. "I will tell you that I was born poor. I've had a very, very, very tough life. That early experience has influenced me in everything I have done. So perhaps I have my childhood to thank for where I am today."

Her lips took a mordant twist. "I'll tell you something else. I've seen enough of the horror of war in all its aspects—bombing, cruelty, hunger—to know that I'll leave the waging of war to others. I want no part of it."

"I had hoped to encourage you to play at least a part in this particular little war. I want you to wage a war of words for us."

Visual salvos fired from eyes the color of a flame's pale blue center. "You have no right to ask that of me," she replied.

The isle of Rhodes resembled an archeological jewel set in the aquamarine sea. Bronze deer atop twin columns flanked the entrance to Mandraki harbor. Before sailing the yawl farther up the island's coast to Lindos, Damon pointed out where the Colossus of Rhodes, one of the Seven Wonders of the Ancient World, had once stood.

The medieval-looking town of Lindos was a picturesque jumble of snow white cubes and domes and cupolas. Against the setting sun, the windows of the port shone gold against the white-washed buildings that covered the dry hillside. On a hill above the town were the ruins of a ramparted castle.

When the yawl was moored at the pier, Damon took Sigourney's hand and helped her onto the dock. The harbor water was brightly painted with the reflections of dories and tavernas, and it was to one of these quaint inns that he took her.

"Dinner first, then a tour of the town's claim to fame," he promised with a smile, and she could tell he was making an effort to be polite and pleasant.

Her initial response was to be petulant, almost childish, to declare that the tour was his idea after all. If she did that, though, he might just call off the plans he had made. He might even send her back. With a shock, she had to acknowledge that she didn't want to leave. So she returned his smile, saying brightly, "I'd like that."

How quickly she was learning humility under his tutelage. It was definitely a new and not altogether pleasant experience.

In the taverna's courtyard, fragrant with orange blossoms, sat sea-weathered fishermen, and women in black dresses who were jesting with modish young people, the backpackers and jetsetters. Damon chose a table that faced the bead-curtained doorway and ordered for both of them.

While they waited for the meal, she noted that he kept the conversation impersonal, and that his eyes were constantly scanning the holiday-goers. She guessed, too, that his ear was atuned to the babble of the many foreign tongues. All his senses were hyperalert. Did he ever relax, let down his guard?

The waiter brought the specialty of the house, jellied pork, followed by *dolmades*, tender grape leaves stuffed with meat and rice. The staple of the tavern was the golden wine called retsina, which she had always thought tasted suspiciously like turpentine.

"*Yassou*," Damon said, lifting his glass. "Your health."

One swallow and her tongue felt like chenille. Noticing the glass that she left over half-filled, he said, smiling, "You don't acquire a taste for retsina. You acquire a tolerance for it."

She noted that as he went on to tell her about the island's sights and history, he finished off his own glass with no apparent harm to his cast-iron system.

"That castle you saw on the hill above Lindos was built in the thirteen hundreds by the Crusaders, the Knights of St. John of Jerusalem. When the Turkish ruler Suleiman the Magnificent laid siege, the knights were vastly outnumbered. Though they were forced to surrender, they fought so valiantly that they were permitted to escape with their lives."

As he spoke of the fighting, a brooding quality darkened his deep blue eyes. She could recall the horrors and deprivations of war, but they were a thing of the past. What did she know of the high-stress conditions under which he constantly worked and lived? She had come to accept her personal freedom as her just due. Damon could not take even that for granted.

To tease him from his brooding, she said lightly, "Did you know, Damon, that your eyes are so dark they're almost black? It must take an enormous amount of light to fill them."

At that, he smiled. She would have preferred that he laugh.

"Come on," he said, sprinkling a handful of drachmas on the table. "We have a town to tour."

Evening was tinting the white of the day a soft blue by the time they left her carry-on with the taverna owner and made their way to the main street. From the shadowy interiors of coffeehouses came the click of dice and dominoes, and the shuffling of cards, interrupted by high-spirited laughter and outbursts of rapidly spoken Greek.

Below, the arcade lights around the harbor winked enticingly. Ahead, gently curving, rose a narrow street of stone steps, bordered by elegantly carved doors, vine-trellised courtyards and the tiny shops of cobblers.

Damon's large hand engulfed hers as he led her up the steep street. She knew she would have to be content with that gesture, one that went further than the normal bounds of a truce to define the tenuous beginnings of friendship.

At intervals windows spilled light into their path, and the fragrance of roasting lamb or the jangling of a bouzouki proclaimed the evening pleasures inside the cottages. They left the houses and shops behind as the path climbed sharply, then swung abruptly to skirt a precipice, hidden by wind-bent trees.

"Damon, where are you taking me?" she demanded as her breath dwindled rapidly.

"To see the ruins of the Temple of Athena, the Virgin." His breathing was effortless. "It's a must on every tour, didn't you know?"

There was no air left in her lungs to reply.

"During the three days of full moon each month," he continued easily, "it is possible to visit the temple after dark, the best time to see it."

Her heart pounded more heavily now, not just from the haste of the climb, but from the splendor of the scene that appeared before her. The temple's superlative sculptures and marbled, fluted columns were moon-bathed, every line expressive of the sense of perfection and beauty that had been the hallmark of the finest architecture ever produced.

High in the east, dodging among clouds, rode the same full moon that must have looked down on other couples who made the climb, seeking the magic of the solitude. She smelled the thyme and camomile that pervaded the air…and felt the touch of Damon's warm flesh against her own.

"It was worth the climb," she whispered. "It makes everything else, the rest of the world and its problems, fade into insignificance."

His hand cupped her shoulder, and she looked up at him. She saw passion in his eyes, but his wanting of her seemed to be mingled inextricably with restraint. With a start, she realized that he was aware of her feelings for him, understood them better, perhaps, than she did.

"The Lazeroses—our hosts while we are here—will be waiting for us," he said. "We had better go."

The Lazeros house in the old quarter of Lindos surprisingly bridged a narrow street. A zigzag stairway led up to the entrance and the flat roof offered a work and lounging space, even serving as a footpath to the other houses that buttressed it.

Sotoris Lazeros was built like a fiddle bow, short and limber. A handlebar mustache almost concealed his swarthy face. His wife, Sophia, was taller, stouter, yet attractive in an indefinable way. Sigourney guessed their ages as mid-thirties.

Sotoris was a sculptor, and his stone-cutting tools, variously shaped chisels and mallets, littered the outer room that served as a gallery for his work. The couple greeted her with the natural reserve that Hellenes had for foreigners. Still, she sensed an underlying warmth, especially in the couple's two young daughters, who flung themselves at Damon. They couldn't have been more than four and five years old.

Brown curls bouncing, they held fast to his arms as he tossed each one to a perch atop either shoulder. If Sigourney hadn't seen it, she wouldn't have believed it—the sight of the forbidding warrior playing Colossus of Rhodes to the little girls and actually laughing with them.

"Off to bed," Sophie told her daughters. With cupid-bow mouths making moues, the little ones deserted their giant playmate. When they were safely tucked in, Sophie led the guests into the kitchen, where she set out coffee cups on a rickety table.

Over the thick, syrupy Turkish coffee that Sigourney thought she would never grow accustomed to, Damon peppered the husband and wife with questions, some of which were asked too rapidly for Sigourney to follow.

At the last question, the wife made a sound through her teeth like "tss," lifted her eyebrows and tossed her head, the classic gesture of nodding up that Hellenes used for saying no.

Damon's dark brows flared upward; then his lids narrowed, shuttering whatever expression had been in his eyes, but his mouth was set tight at the corners. Sigourney cast him a questioning look, but he offered no explanation.

The conversation flowed rapidly back and forth between Damon and the other two, and with her memory of Greek gradually returning from the enforced exposure, Sigourney was able to participate occasionally. She could catch the gist of a joke and share their laughter, although it seemed a bit forced to her. Damon smiled occasionally, but never laughed.

A little later, Sophie showed her to the room where she would sleep that night. It was small and cozy, with a hand-knitted spread draped over the white iron bedstead. Hanging in a niche above the bed was an icon of the Virgin.

"Tomorrow you can sleep late," Damon said when Sophie had gone.

He set her bag just inside the doorway, but when he turned to leave she asked, "Where are you sleeping?"

"On the roof. It's much cooler there."

The only place left, too, she thought. She didn't want him to leave. "Damon, earlier tonight...what was it Sophie said that made you look so—I don't know—so hard, so cold?"

For a long moment he looked at her, hands on his hips, and she knew he was trying to decide what he would tell her. "Uncle Naxos—the fisherman who met us with the yawl..."

"Yes?"

"He was found this evening in the trunk of the Fiat, bound and gagged. He had been shot through the temple after being tortured."

The ancient fear rattled up and down her spine like a worn zipper. "Dear God!" Her mind snailed forward through its morass of horror to digest the afterthought.

"Damon, he was more than your uncle, he was almost your father!"

She saw the grim eyes begin to shut down, a fan of lines radiating from the outer corners. "I have seen death before." The rich voice dropped the words like a bomb into the stillness of the little room.

Stunned, she backed away until her calves brushed against the bed and prevented further retreat. "Don't you see?" she whispered. "By fighting, you become the thing you're fighting against. You become indifferent to death and suffering."

His hands clenched and his face twisted before he spun on his heel and left.

Deep in the night, she cried out in her sleep. Shrapnel exploded about her. Someone, another abandoned child, ran past her, his body a torch of fire. She ran, too. From what, she did not know. Instinct told her to run, to catch up with the fleeing civilians. She was alone, and Death in the form of a gray battle tank rolled behind her, slowly gaining on her....

"Noooo! Nooo! Hel-l-lp meee. Hel-l-lp mee!"

A sound dug into his unconsciousness, jerking him awake. He heard a cadence, without really hearing individual words. What he heard could have been the steady, angry beat of his heart. Drawn by something beyond his ken, he rose from the pallet and padded across the roof to the stairwell, where the whimper of a frightened child could be clearly heard.

He moved to her doorway, his eyes focusing on the restlessly thrashing woman on the moonlit bed, her ebony hair twisted on the pillow. Sheened with perspiration, her flesh made him think of flowing honey, translucent gold. He longed to taste it.

Strangely, though, he was angered, too, by her sweet-smelling skin, so clean and fresh. So American. It had never been soiled by the degradation of prison life. She was almost incandescent, with that ageless look of people who have survived a holocaust.

He crossed to the bed and shook her gently. "Sigourney. Sigourney. Wake up. It's all right. I am here."

Eyelids weighted by dense lashes slowly eased open. Looking into her pale blue eyes was like diving deep, deep, into the depths of a cool tropical sea. He could lose himself there and oh so easily lose his very purpose.

"Damon," she whispered. "Please, hold me. Just hold me."

His temples tightened. He sat beside her and gathered her against him. His olive skin was a counterpoint to her rich golden color. He could feel her lashes tangled in the wiry hair of his chest; he could feel her pulse pounding against his flesh. A yearning was reborn in him after a long, long period of ashen loneliness.

He grew hard with her warmth against him, even as he felt the slow, almost refractive change in her breathing. He simply couldn't give her what she wanted, and he dropped his hands away and faced her numbly.

"Are you all right now?"

Wide-eyed, she nodded, and he left her and returned to the roof and his own private hell.

Chapter 4

Sigourney woke with no memory of the nightmare and, incredibly, without a thought of Damon in her mind, without anything beyond a general feeling of good will and buoyancy.

It wasn't until she was dressing, wriggling into a vibrant orange sundress, that he slipped casually into the back of her mind, then leaped in an instant to the forefront with a force that brought her up short.

What he had done for her the night before—the comfort he had afforded her, asking nothing, taking nothing, only giving—altered her perception of him. She sensed that there was a reserve in him somewhere, that she was seeing only the tip of a very large and complicated iceberg. That feeling made her even more vulnerable to him, a development she simply couldn't afford.

She sat on the bed, a flimsy sandal in one hand, and contemplated just what she was about. The anticipation of seeing Damon again, of being with him, was strong and sweet. But into the joyous image of his comfort last night slithered a crumpled, bloody body stuffed into a tiny car trunk.

Damon was a political outlaw; any involvement with him, other than the most superficial, could only lead her into a hornet's nest of problems, one of which was that merely associating with him automatically linked her with his underground organization and could subject her to Agamemnon's bloodthirsty reprisal. The fact that she was a reporter or an American be damned.

Another problem was Damon's total dedication to the PFF—obviously, it led to a dead-end street; then, too, he had been married before, which meant a host of other problems. She didn't want to let herself think about these things. She would simply enjoy the week, keeping her relationship with Damon on the most casual basis.

She finished dressing, completing her ensemble with a short jacket that matched the tiered sundress. She roped her mass of hair into a knot atop her head as a precaution against the sticky heat the day would certainly bring. Then she went to greet the Lazeroses.

Sotoris rose from a kneeling position before an unfinished stone sculpture and greeted her with a smile. "I hope the pounding of my mallet did not disturb you," he said, his handlebar mustache lifting and falling with the rhythm of his words.

"Not at all." She smiled. "In fact, I'm afraid I've overslept. I'm usually up long before this."

The children were nowhere in sight, but in the kitchen, primitive by Western standards, Sophie courteously offered her coffee and a sesame-seed roll called a *koulouria*. The woman's hands and face were powdered with a light dusting of flour from the dough she was kneading.

Sigourney took a wake-up sip of the thick, strong coffee and asked Sophie, "Is Damon up yet?"

The woman paused in her kneading and wiped her hands on her apron. "He was gone at dawn, when we awakened." She crossed to the chipped porcelain enamel sideboard and picked up a folded scrap of paper. "He left us a note saying that if you awoke before he returned I was to give you this."

When did the man sleep? Sigourney wondered. It had been long after midnight when they went to bed, and even then he had been up during the night, comforting her.

She unfolded the paper. Sophie busied herself with the bread dough. From the other room came the heavy thud of mallet against chisel against reluctant stone.

The note contained no salutation; only a neatly penned message: *If you feel you have seen all you want, Sotoris will take you to the harbor where you can catch a ferry back to the mainland. If not, I will return by ten to show you the rest of the island.*

In other words, he was telling her that if Naxos's death had frightened her off, she was free to leave. She was tempted to do just that. However, the possibility that Damon would know just how weak she was tugged her conscience the other way. She was driven by a little bit of shame and more than a little bit of desire to see him again.

She refolded the piece of paper, tucked it inside her skirt pocket and poured another cup of coffee. She decided it wasn't so bad, really. She must be getting used to it. It did have the taste of swamp, though.

After she finished the coffee, she helped Sophie with the morning dishes. Sophie was telling her about the chic new shops and the disco—a first for the island—that had opened down at the quay, when Sigourney heard Damon talking in the other room with Sotoris. That deep, melodic voice was like a magnet, but she denied the urge to run to him, to feast her eyes on his handsome face and bask in his presence.

When he appeared in the doorway, she turned with a calm, amiable smile. "Hi," she said. "Do you happen to have a cigarette?"

Typically, his expression was contained. She couldn't tell if he was surprised or pleased or annoyed that she was still there. "Turkish, as usual." He reached in his shirt pocket and offered her one from the pack.

After he lit her cigarette, he said to Sophie, "You don't happen to have any *kreatopita* left over to pack for a lunch for us, do you?"

A grin of pleasure made the woman's features extraordinarily pretty. "I make the best *kreatopita* on the island, eh?"

"The best!"

Sigourney envied the affectionate smile Damon awarded the woman.

After he made arrangements for Sotoris to stow the picnic basket aboard the fishing yawl, Damon took her down to the marketplace.

Lighthearted young invaders from Western Europe and the United States, beaded and bearded, crowded the narrow avenues of stalls. She saw young couples and old holding hands as they roamed through the maze of offerings, but Damon did not attempt to hold hers. The night before, when he had held her close to him, might never have happened, might instead have been a part of her dream.

"Oriste! Oriste!" cried the merchants. "What will you have?"

What would she have, indeed? A worn-out fire hose? A mandolin? An oil lamp, a goat bell, an old coin?

"Come and see!" invited a vendor. "Everything good and cheap!"

About the shouts of the hawkers, the arguing of the customers and the shuffling of feet, the air trembled with the discordant assault of phonographs. Sigourney heard the Oriental wail of Turkish music, the brassy blare of a Latin-American dance band, the throaty growl of a jazz singer, the tinkle of a bouzouki and someone singing a love ballad in French.

On a side street, they wandered through mountains of tomatoes from Crete, olives from Cyprus, lemons from Patras, and blood oranges from Istanbul. Iced bins of red mullet and crayfish and lobsters revealed the islanders' chief occupation. The market's aromas were foreign to her, and the fruits and vegetables oddly shaped.

Square in the middle of the market Damon pointed to a customer sitting on a box to get his mustache trimmed. Around the man others were gathered to talk. "You see," Damon told her, "conversation is a favorite pastime. The Hellenic word for marketplace, *agora,* comes from the same root as *agorena*—'I make a speech.'"

He stopped at one stall and purchased a blue beaded necklace for her. The necklace was inexpensive but artistically crafted. "It's claimed the blue beads ward off the evil eye," he said with a hint of a smile.

She wished he'd smile more often. But he was a private man and, she sensed, one who strove to contain an almost seething impatience. Was he frustrated by his role as her tour guide?

While the sightseers and shoppers streamed by, he fastened the necklace about her neck, his fingers deft though his hands were so large.

"You've been a perfect host," she said over her shoulder. "I've been half expecting you to launch your campaign to proselytize me with PFF doctrine."

He clasped her shoulders and turned her to fix her with a skeptical gaze. "I do not think you are ready to hear or see the unpleasant side of Macedonian life."

"You're right. I'm not. I'm on a holiday."

Never in her life had she responded to a man as she had to Damon. Why, she couldn't imagine. He had all the finesse of a Patton tank. He was arrogant and entirely too

sure of himself. Even now, he stood at ease with that
calmness of big men who have nothing to prove.

"Then let us continue with the tour," he said with that
civility that grated on her so.

When he arranged for them to take a donkey ride up
the steep cliffs to the Shrine of St. Paul, her pique was
converted quickly into laughter. Damon had to lift his
long legs high to keep his shoes from dragging in the
rocky dust.

During the half-hour trip they alternated between
pulling the sturdy little beasts along the track and
whacking them on the rear with switches. Occasionally
the animals became the masters, which resulted in off-
trail meandering and a few impromptu races.

As they approached the shrine, she slid from her donkey's back and collapsed, breathless with laughter, into
Damon's outstretched arms. "I have to commend you,"
he told her, grinning. "You are becoming an intrepid
tourist."

Shyness knotted her tongue. Praise was rare from him.
She extricated herself from the danger his embrace
promised and managed to ask calmly, "Well, are you
going to show me around?"

As they drew apart, he seemed as relieved as she.
Leaving the donkeys to graze on the orphaned tufts of
grass poking up here and there, he led her to a little white
chapel surrounded by towering trees that must have been
saplings when St. Paul visited the island.

Beneath a tree's waterfall of leaves a grandmother of
a woman sat, winding yarn made of wool that had been

soaked in the sea to take out the oil and odor, and then bleached and spun. Sigourney guessed the old woman served as the shrine's watchman. The chapel's wooden doors, as weather-pitted as the old woman, were open, and inside candles flickered before the altar dedicated to St. Paul's memory.

It was hard to tell how old the chapel was, certainly several hundred years, but there was a serenity within the dim, musty sanctuary. Damon dropped a coin in the wooden box at the door and picked up an unlit candle from the table. From the rear of the chapel, she watched as he left her to kneel at the altar. Lighting his candle from the flame of another, he set it in an empty socket and bowed his tawny head.

She couldn't have been more astonished. She would have classified him as nonreligious. Was that where his power came from? How long since she had offered up her own prayers? Too long. Months.

Looking at his broad back, she felt like an intruder, so she quietly left the chapel. Outside, the white sunlight was blinding. She remained in the shadows of the shrine and watched the old woman wind the yarn. In a few minutes, Damon joined her. The tension and anger usually held in check by his great intelligence were noticeably absent.

"I think it is time we ate our lunch," he said. "I thought you would enjoy a picnic on the other side of the island. It is seldom visited, and there are ruins of Byzantine mosques and early Christian churches."

Down at the harbor, tourists and holiday-festive couples listened to strolling musicians or sampled the incomparable local seafood, and fishermen repaired their nets. With Sophie's picnic basket stowed in the yawl's stern, Damon guided the boat out to sea.

The day was lazy and warm, and getting to be hot, too, so Sigourney was content to settle back and watch the bay slide from sight as the yawl coasted around a promontory that gave a splendid view of spectacular cliffs. For mile after mile, sheer granite rose three thousand feet or more from the crashing surf. Then the wall of rock became even craggier, and here and there magnificent waterfalls tumbled into the sea far below.

By squinting her eyes against the sun's glare, she could just make out white goats scampering lithely up cliffs and across ledges that no man could possibly negotiate.

She was savoring the peacefulness of the moment. She respected Damon's stillness, realizing that he wasn't ready to talk. Yet another part of her wanted him to open up, so she could probe this uncommon man with such potent, private emotions. There was such a calm ease, such a sureness, about him. What had gone into the making of him? She wanted to ask him about his wife. Did he still care deeply for her? Or could he ever care deeply for anyone?

She closed her eyes and drowsed until the deceleration of the yawl's engine let her know that they would be reaching shore soon.

A verdant peninsula jutted out from the coast, and he put in there. It was a lovely spot, with grassy shores where one could look west and east toward the majestic cliffs. Remnants of marble blocks and broken shafts of Corinthian columns crowned the peninsula's center, the site of some ancient pagan temple.

Basket in one hand, Damon touched her elbow with the other and guided her up the boulder-strewn slope. His fingers at her elbow stirred a roiling sensation in the pit of her stomach. At a clear area, tiled by a floor of weathered and chipped mosaics, he relinquished her from the sensuality of his touch to open the picnic basket. Sophie had even thought to include a blue linen tablecloth, along with a bottle of the inevitable retsina to wash down the chopped veal that had been fried in a crust.

Perched on a broken column, a large pelican rattled his beak, closely inspecting the items Damon withdrew from the basket. Sigourney's soft laughter drew the seabird's attention before it was diverted by screeching overhead and deserted the humans and their lunch for its own kind.

"How did you meet the Lazeroses?" she asked between bites of flaky *kreatopita*.

"We three are from the same village. When Agamemnon began his purge of unsympathetic Macedonians, Sophie and Sotoris escaped to Rhodes."

He passed her the bottle, and she drank straight from its mouth, as he had done, a gesture that seemed to her one of intimacy. The retsina still tasted god-awful. "And they're part of your underground network?"

"Among other things, they act as intermediaries in the few shipments of weapons that we are able to smuggle into Macedonia." His eyes challenged her. "Are you interested in knowing more?"

Yes, she wanted to know more about this extraordinary man. But not about his mission. She did not like being drawn into Damon Demetrios's strange world of secrecy and terror. However, Damon and his involvement—no, dedication was a better word—with the PFF seemed inseparable. Well then, she would beat Damon Demetrios at his own game, in her way.

"All right," she said crisply, calculatingly, "what can this 'army of self-defense' possibly hope to accomplish?"

"We act as an unseen force in restraining Agamemnon's repressive dictatorship and ultimately in negotiating with the United Nations."

"Attacks on radar installations and military storehouses aren't always bloodless. Don't you feel a political nausea because of your activities?"

"No."

Ahh, so he refused to engage in a verbal battle. "Then, do you feel fear?"

He set the left-over veal aside and laced his hands between wide-spread knees. "I have nothing to lose in what I undertake."

He paused, and she knew something was going on behind the unrevealing blue of his dark eyes; they hid a part of him that he would never let outsiders glimpse. "Sometimes...after a dangerous mission is over and nothing has happened, I feel twice alive. A feeling of exhilaration that comes only from cheating death—or from creating life, making love."

A cynical smile twisted her lips. "That's rather an old-fashioned phrase, isn't it—'making love'?"

He looked at her steadily. "I can speak only for myself."

With a bizarre feeling of jealousy, she wondered who the woman was who knew the depths of this man's passion. Had only the spectral wife experienced the depths of sensual intensity of which Sigourney suspected him capable? She felt that loving him would be like reaching out in a desperate attempt to touch him across a vast, dark, empty space. How many women had longed to taste his intensity and failed? Damon ran deep and still. A woman would have to change her whole psyche, her whole life, for him.

Despite the shimmering heat of the summer afternoon, she shivered, and he asked, "Finished?"

Was he asking about the lunch or her interest in him? He had left the choice to her, so she said, "Yes."

He shrugged those bull-like shoulders and began to gather up the remnants of the picnic and put them in the basket. In an electrified silence she helped him.

She had thought they would be returning to Lindos immediately, but unexpectedly he brought the yawl into a cove walled by towering rock and decorated by a glistening, multiprismed waterfall. He killed the engine. "Let's go for a swim."

She started to say something about her lack of a swimsuit, then felt terribly young and foolish and gauche. "I'd like that," she said sedately. "But I don't normally parade naked in front of a stranger."

Damon cocked his head, studying her. "Your maidenly modesty is unexpected. You are a thirty-seven-year-old woman—of uncommon beauty."

"You seem to know a great deal about me. Are you asking how many lovers I've had?"

His teeth flashed white against the sun-golden shade of his skin. "That fact was not covered in any of the articles we compiled about you."

"Shall I ask the same of you?"

He stripped off his shirt to bare his massive chest. "I have never kept count."

"And I don't need to."

How could she admit that over a span of nearly forty years only a couple of men had ever inspired in her that passion called love? She had never known a love that demanded such an intense and total commitment of mind and soul as would be required in a relationship with Damon. But then, she had never encountered a man like him.

She might be intrinsically shy, but she was certainly not naive. She had lived too long in a fast-paced world of international intrigue and power and wealth, had fended off too many men, to be disconcerted by a man trying to put the make on her. Yet Damon and his taut control put her at a disadvantage and confused her.

"I would have thought you too much an honest woman," he said, "to play coy games."

She accepted the taunt and reached for the sundress's side zipper. The dress slithered down about her ankles.

Clad only in lacy briefs, she unflinchingly met his stare. His own trousers lay in a heap at his feet.

They measured each other. He was as fit as an Olympic athlete. His thighs and calves were incredibly muscled, as were his arms. Big. That was all she could think of in terms of description. And beautiful, if that could be said of a man. His briefs could not conceal the bold evidence of his desire. Her visual assessment faltered.

Belatedly, she wondered what he thought of her. Her breasts were full and firm, but small, at least compared to the buxom females of that part of Europe. The rest of her body was, she supposed, like any other woman's; maybe her legs were longer and her panty-clad derriere quite neatly curved, but was that enough to make him find her any more appealing than any number of attractive women who would desire him?

Did she really want to risk an affair with Damon and its accompanying consequences, to become entangled in the imbroglio of his life?

Before his appreciative gaze she lifted her arms and removed the pins from her hair, a deliberate attempt to buy time. She imagined that with her hair tumbling loose and the primitive necklace lying between her bared breasts, she must resemble some kind of pagan.

Embarrassed by both the thought and her state of nudity, she dove smoothly into the crystal clear sea. The water was refreshingly cool. Surfacing, she called out to him, "Race you to the falls!"

Once she chanced a look behind her. He still stood on the yawl, his arms akimbo, laughing. The sight—Damon actually laughing—almost took her breath away. Then his body carved the blue-green waters, and she had to concentrate on the race.

Quickly it became more than just a race. It became a contest of two powerful wills. Her cupped hands sliced cleanly through the rippling waters, propelling her forward, matching her metronomelike kick, but not quickly enough. She could sense him gaining, could hear the steady splashing of his mighty legs, thrusting him nearer with each stroke. As she drew closer to the falls, the roar of their cascading water overcame all other noise.

Suddenly her ankle was caught and yanked backward. She slipped beneath the sea's surface, down, down through the cool, shimmering, watery depths. Damon's hands slid over her thighs to grasp her waist, propelling her upward along with him. They broke water, gasping, laughing.

"You cheated!" she charged, shouting to make herself heard above the splash from the falls.

"You set no rules."

The waterfalls' spray pummeled them as he drew her along with smooth backstrokes until they were behind its torrential curtain. Lodged between him and the underledge of rock, she no longer had to tread water. How good he felt against her. In that silvery wonderworld she was sharply aware of her naked breasts, cold and turgid, pressed into the diamond patch of golden curls that covered his chest. Her smoldering gaze darted up to his glistening face. His eyes blazed, but his fingers were gentle

as they brushed aside the long, wet strands of hair clinging to her lips.

For a man who led a violent life, his lips moved so
tenderly over hers. His tongue demanded no entry, but he
seemed to take great pleasure simply from mapping with
his lips the contours of hers. His arms at either side of her
were so strong. She exchanged kiss for kiss, touch for
touch, with an abandon she had never known.

She quickly became aware of the sensual excitement
building relentlessly in her and knew she was in immi-
nent danger of losing herself to him. Instinct told her that
what was happening had not been planned, was acciden-
tal. She suspected that he was as surprised as she was by
the unexpected fury of their passion. When his palm deserted her cheek to caress the column of her neck, a small
knot pulsed spasmodically in the pit of her stomach.

She made no protest when his huge hand continued its
downward course to completely cover one breast. Under
the pressure of his fingers, her nipples stiffened inde-
pendently of one another. He lowered his mouth to nib-
ble one, his tongue smooth and rough like a cat's, and as
he did, a gasp zephyred through her parted lips.

In that prismed, pristine sea place, the world spun in
slow motion, time had no ending, space was an infinity.

The hand that kneaded her breast made her feel reck-
less and a shimmer of heat formed between her legs as he
thrust insistently against her thigh.... Her tongue darted
out to touch and play with his, tasting the saltwater that
mingled within the vacuum of their mouths.... His fin-

gers slid further downward to cup the nylon-shielded delta of her thighs, and her head tilted back to rest against the granite wall.... His mouth was buried in the hollow of her neck.... Like a purring feline she arched her hips into his large palm, feeling with a quickness of breath the fingers pressed against her.... Foolishly, she felt faint...her **bre**athing ragged....

At her ear, his breath was hot, his tongue persuasive. "Sigourney, I want you."

She shook her head, not in a negative gesture, but in an attempt to find in the erotic infinity in which she was trapped a semblance of sanity.

Her effort was futile. She was beyond helping herself. She could only float acquiescently within the support of his arm while he stripped away their underwear. Then he was moving against her, and she yielded to that primeval insistence, spreading her legs, offering herself, taking him inside her.

Rhythmically he plunged and withdrew, and the force of water first filling her and then rushing out triggered explosions of neon lights behind her lids and left her gasping. The drugs and tricks that the sexually jaded resorted to could not have excited her more. Pinned against the water-smoothed ledge, she writhed within the throes of inarticulate passion. She nipped at his thick neck like a wild mare in heat.

This loss of self was so unlike Sigourney. She knew she would regret what she was doing as soon as the act was finished, but she was powerless to deny the need he had engendered in her.

He shuddered against her, his essence mingling with the sea, and she was at last released from the age-old rite. After a moment he raised his head. Brutal sunlight reflected off his wet skin and eyelashes, where water drops clung. She saw in his eyes that for him it had been little more than that lusty coming together of two people who haven't yet come to know each other.

His inquiring gaze held hers until she looked away in shame. His obvious lack of emotional involvement contrasted startlingly with her own confusion that had been growing since the moment they met. "Please...this was wrong," she mumbled. "It should never have happened."

The water lapped coldly about them, seeping into the minute space that suddenly separated his body from hers. He didn't speak.

She pushed herself away from the rocky wall and swam with unsteady but increasingly deliberate strokes back to the undulating boat, then pulled herself over the gunwale. If he hadn't wanted to let her go, she never could have escaped from those powerful arms. Behind her, he climbed aboard the yawl. He slipped into and zippered his trousers, all the time watching her struggling with the now-damp sundress. The gentle slap of the wavelets against the boat's hull was the only sound in the loud silence.

She broke it. "I don't do things like this, Damon, and casually leave afterward." With an impatient movement of her head, she tossed the wet hair back from her face. "I can't...don't...leave a trail of affairs in my wake."

"I do not have time to play word games, Sigourney. I know you wanted me, as I wanted you. We are not two teenagers groping in the back seat of a car."

She was embarrassed. She had been melodramatic. And...she was a little frightened of her response to this man, frightened by her lack of control. She averted her eyes from the brushfire of his. "I wish I were sixteen again and things were that uncomplicated."

"The tides of this sea are treacherous, and only the strongest swimmers can survive."

She whirled on him, her orange sundress held over her breasts. The slashing line of his mouth twitched at a modesty that had come a bit too late. "That's just it!" she gritted. "I'm not brave. Oh, my words are, my writing is. But *I'm* not, Damon. I can't follow the simple, uncluttered rules that govern your war-filled world, where you go to bed with someone if you desire him because tomorrow may not come."

"I suppose it's unchivalrous of me to point out that you just did...what you did for no other reason than natural passion," he said, his words icily spaced.

"You don't have to remind me," she hurled back. She took a deep breath and added, "It's something that I already regret, and I'll probably continue to do so for some time to come—if I let myself think about you that long."

That evening she left Rhodes on the ferry to Constantine, and somewhere in the ferry's frothy wake floated the blue bead necklace before it sank from sight.

Chapter 5

The white-kilted, red-capped *evzones* no longer flanked the French doors; now they stood stiffly at attention on either side of Sigourney's chair. With apparent calmness, she sat with her chin resting on her fist, while Agamemnon paced before her. His normally florid complexion was pale, drained by the adrenaline-fueled rage coursing through him. In one hand he held her passport, which had been lifted, along with her press ID's, when one of the *evzones* had rifled her purse.

She picked a nonexistent piece of lint from her black matte jersey and said, "One of your VASIK agents escorted me here, General. Would you be so kind as to explain why? Surely I didn't forget the date of our next interview, did I?"

He fingered the passport and looked down at her with a smile, but a malignant quality spoiled it and left her chilled. She didn't need to remind herself that this was a man of exceptional cunning and brute force.

"You surprised me, Miss Hamilton. I gave you more credit than this—to let yourself become involved with revolutionaries."

"Isn't that precisely what you once were, General?"

The lids dropped halfway over his eyes. "You were accorded all the privileges of the press, Miss Hamilton! You were welcomed here at the Royal Palace, trusted. Yet my agent reports that you have consorted with antinationals, terrorists who would undermine and destroy Macedonia."

He paused, as if giving her an opportunity to refute the charge of complicity with terrorists.

"Do you have a cigarette, General? I hope it's an American brand. I really don't care too much for Turkish tobacco."

His eyelids jitterbugged, and she fought to keep from laughing hysterically. "You will be on the next flight out of Constantine, Miss Hamilton! I cannot be responsible for your safety if you remain. Do you understand?" Agamemnon's tirade was all the more menacing because he delivered it in a stage whisper.

Fury rattled up and down her spine. She rose, tucking her purse under one arm. If only she had Damon's self-containment. At the thought of him, she felt another kind of anger. At times over the past twenty-four hours she had found herself loathing the man.

She stared Agamemnon down. "I understand you implicitly, General. I believe it's called repression of freedom of the press."

Agamemnon's mouth twisted into a feral baring of his yellowish teeth. "As I said, it is for your own safety. Unpleasant things can happen to a woman alone in Macedonia. Especially during the madness of Midsummer Midnight Week. Your passport will be waiting for you when you board the plane."

He was keeping her passport! Her talisman against all harm. Not until that precise moment did she realize the gravity of her situation. How could this have happened? Fear iced the blood in her veins. She was about to try to persuade him to change his mind, to remind him that she was an American citizen and a member of the press, when he nodded curtly at the *evzones* and she found herself quickly flanked by the two men. As they escorted her toward the double doors, she caught a glimpse of her reflection in the large beveled mirror. She wouldn't have recognized herself. Her face was chalk white, her expression wooden, numbed by disbelief.

From the other side of the two-way mirror, Kopeta watched the woman being escorted from Agamemnon's office. Beside the VASIK colonel's chair the intercom buzzed, and Agamemnon's voice barked, "Have her taxi followed. And make certain she gets on that plane."

Kopeta's flat face registered none of the contempt he felt for the general, whom he considered as having too big an ego for his small size. It was Kopeta's conviction that men like Agamemnon often overlooked the little things like resentment, which could tumble them for their thrones just as surely as large-scale rebellions.

Had it been Kopeta's decision, he would have ordered the female reporter terminated at once.

As the taxi took her back to her hotel for her belongings, Sigourney decided that Agamemnon was right in one respect, at least. The end of the week was rapidly approaching and, as he predicted, would culminate in the madness of Midsummer Midnight. Though it was only noon, her taxi crept along the wide boulevard, choked now with costumed revelers taking the opportunity to enjoy the government's laxity during the national holiday.

It was a virtual Mardi Gras. A roly-poly man pinned in an enormous diaper paraded past the car's front bumper. Outside her window, six people dressed as beer bottles and bound together in a replica of a beer carton walked along in shaky unison.

She might have momentarily enjoyed the spectacle, but she had the instinctive certainty that she was being followed. A quick glance over her shoulder confirmed the feeling. The driver in the car immediately behind wore an orange sweatshirt—like the sweatshirt worn by one of the men who had watched her and Damon through binoculars from the cliff that day.

She leaned forward and told her driver, "Please, I'm in a hurry; can you take an alternate route around all this?"

The driver nodded and made a turn at the next intersection, but there the traffic was blocked by a military parade. Though people lined the curbs, only a little cheering and tooting of horns was taking place. When the parade reached Constantine's grand plaza, Agamemnon himself would address the people from the Royal Palace balcony.

She turned around to check her pursuer. He was still behind her. Suddenly a loud crackle of fireworks erupted. To the right of her taxi, a man in a clown suit who was watching the parade dropped to the pavement. At first Sigourney assumed he was merely drunk. Then a soldier staggered from the march formation. Crimson splotched his stomach. Another soldier pitched forward.

It was gunfire she had heard, not firecrackers!

"MPA!" the taxi driver warned and ducked below the dashboard.

Chaos swept through the ranks of parading soldiers. Some went down on one knee and began indiscriminately firing sprays of bullets into the screaming crowd. Others dashed for the cover of buildings and fired with the precision of sharpshooters. Sigourney grabbed the pad and pen from her purse and began jotting notations that were a form of shorthand decipherable only by her.

The taxi's windshield was suddenly starred from a buzzing bullet, and she, too, dropped to the floor. She continued to scribble, describing the attack by the militant Macedonian nationals. The firing became sporadic. Cautiously she levered herself back onto the seat. The half dozen or so terrorists who still crouched behind the cover of buildings and cars were all young—and foolishly full of zeal, she thought sadly. These idealists were the junior warriors recruited by the Macedonian Provisional Army.

With a detachment born both of childhood observation and, later, of professional duty, she recorded the death of a teenage girl in jeans and a T-shirt, one of the remaining terrorists. Still armed, the girl darted into a bastion of soldiers and hurled what must have been a Molotov cocktail before a machine gun stitched her chest with bullets. The fiery explosion disintegrated the human bastion, but with it the attack ended.

So had the life of Sigourney's follower. A quick glance behind gave Sigourney a grisly view of the man slumped over the steering wheel. He had been caught in the crossfire.

An hour later, when a semblance of order had been restored to the area, the taxi driver took Sigourney on to her hotel. She sat in the back seat, trying to shake off the tragedy she had witnessed. She reminded herself that she had a plane to catch. She was leaving, and nothing was going to stop her. If Damon had showed the slightest sign of really caring, she might not have had the strength to go. But the thought of his steely coldness strengthened her determination to resist, to leave him to his precious cause.

When she opened her hotel room door, she discovered that she had a visitor, who had apparently been watching the street fighting from her vantage point at the window. The woman turned a lovely, heart-shaped face to Sigourney and studied her with calm intent.

The flood of afternoon sun highlighted a network of faint, fine lines at the corners of the woman's eyes. Her blond hair was cut stylishly short and lightened by an invasion of silver strands. She looked vaguely familiar to Sigourney.

Sigourney shut the door behind her. "I would have sworn I locked my door when I left the room this morning."

"I've been wondering what you'd be like." The woman's voice was well modulated, cultured; the gray pinstriped skirt and jacket were elegantly tailored.

Her visitor's presumption annoyed Sigourney. She leaned against the door of the room and crossed her arms. "I don't suppose you're the room maid. I can think of two other possibilities. You could be the house detective or, conversely, a thief, though I don't think you're either. Furthermore, you have the advantage of knowing my identity. I'd like an explanation."

The woman crossed to the plum brocaded sofa and sat down. Her back was Victorian straight, and she sat forward slightly on the cushions. "Please, sit down."

Sigourney lifted a brow. "I was under the impression this was my room."

The woman bit her bottom lip. "I apologize for my rudeness." For all her composure, the woman's fingertips rubbed lightly against each other, betraying her anxiety. "I am Lady Phillipa Fleming. I wanted to talk with you, and circumstances make it difficult to approach you openly."

Sigourney remembered her now. Years before she had covered the wedding of Princess Anne. This woman had been in the bridal party. A member of British royalty, Lady Phillipa was the offspring of a Greek industrialist's daughter and an English lord, and thus held dual nationality.

Sigourney crossed the thick, plush carpet, and sank into the deep, tufted chair. "All right. I'm listening. Go ahead."

Lady Phillipa looked down at her intertwined fingers, then met Sigourney's stare of curiosity. "It's about Damon Demetrios."

All Sigourney's senses went on red alert. She said nothing.

"The Pan-Hellenic Freedom Forces need your help badly. Your stories could sway public opinion, even persuade reluctant international financiers to back our cause. We're in desperate need of weapons. Our resistance forces in the hills often fight with nothing more than shepherds' staffs."

Flames of fury crackled in Sigourney's head. Damon never gave up. What he couldn't get one way, he'd try to get another. "I thought I made it plain to Damon that I don't support fighting of any kind, even if it's camouflaged in the name of defense."

"Damon didn't send me. He doesn't know I'm here, Miss Hamilton. He's too proud to ask for your help again. I—I hoped maybe I could dissuade you from leaving.''

"Damon can be very persuasive, too, can't he?'' Sigourney said, hating herself for the taunt. She had no reason to want to be rude to this woman. Cattiness had never been one of her traits. "Tell me, what makes you think you can succeed where he couldn't?''

"I'm not sure, really. Damon is so self-sufficient that I'm sure he'll find a way yet to accomplish his purpose. But it's yet another burden for him to shoulder. He already carries too much. So, whatever I can do...'' She lifted her palms expressively.

Sigourney understood. Clearly. Lady Phillipa was obviously in love with Damon. Wanting to know more, and yet not wanting to know, she asked, "Tell me your part in all of this. How did you become involved with Damon?''

Agitation shaded caramel brown eyes that were only lightly made up. The woman hesitated, then said in a low, taut voice, "My husband was president of the university when Agamemnon overthrew the monarchy. I will tell you that my husband is also a Jew.

"Agamemnon's army began rounding up people suspected of antinationalism. One day my husband didn't return home from the university. The next week Agamemnon, in his role as chancellor, appeared in full academic robes for the graduation ceremonies. That same night my husband's body was found. His handkerchief had been stuffed down his throat, and...the rest is simply too grisly to detail. Agamemnon ordered an investigation, of course, but it revealed nothing. Later, an official statement reported that my husband was murdered and robbed by unknown assailants."

Sigourney bit her bottom lip. It was always the same with tyrants—cruel tortures, killer squads, anti-intellectualism, an aggressive war posture, and, above all, racism and bigotry.

"I conducted a vigorous campaign of protest," Lady Phillipa went on, "and soon found myself in prison for thirty-one days. I heard the screams of the tortured and saw...well, I saw things that nightmares and horror movies don't even begin to approach. At that time the United Nations Commission on Human Rights was investigating charges against Agamemnon, and as a gesture of goodwill he released several political prisoners. I—and Damon—were among them. I was stripped of my Macedonian citizenship and was to be deported as an 'undesirable alien.' Instead I hid out and allied myself with the Pan-Hellenic Freedom Forces."

And with Damon, Sigourney thought.

"The university had a distinguished faculty and an excellent reputation. Now it's on the verge of collapse. Many of its professors who were foreign nationals have left. Students are often harassed and killed."

"You belong to the British aristocracy. Can't you raise money from friends and relatives?"

"You know the old story—the impoverished British noblemen who turn their mortgaged country mansions into museums. My mother's Macedonian assets were confiscated when Agamemnon took over. What I'm able to raise is pitifully inadequate.''

Sigourney looked at her watch. She had less than an hour and a half left before her flight was due to leave, and she hadn't begun to pack. Lady Phillipa studied her with anxious eyes.

Sigourney rose to pace the room, her hands hugging her arms as if she were cold. Her journalistic side was infuriated at Agamemnon's tyrannical method of suppressing unfavorable opinions.

Yet her American passport had always been her safeguard. To miss that flight meant surrendering that safeguard.

Then there was Damon. She was furious with him. Even though he was not a member of the MPA, he could still have stopped the senseless killings that afternoon, a demonstration of death that had accomplished nothing but the wasting of young lives.

No, it had accomplished something. She was outraged enough about what had happened to want to do something. And he had known she would be shaken by it! He had known she would either hear about or actually witness the attack, and thus had not interfered.

"Where can I find Damon?" she demanded of her lovely intruder.

Relief flickered in Lady Fleming's eyes.

Chapter 6

Damon has to be the coldest human being I've ever met, Father. He'd stop at nothing to gain his objective. He lives by the bottom line. There isn't an ounce of sympathy or compassion in him. Not a trace. Zilch. The man doesn't know what it means to care, to open himself to weakness. He operates as efficiently and unemotionally as a computer. He doesn't sleep, doesn't eat, doesn't laugh, doesn't cry. He doesn't know the meaning of fear or—"

"You really should try to polish up your skills as an orator, Sigourney. Sermons are for politicians and priests." Father Murphy waggled his thick eyebrows to underscore the intended humor of his remark, and she had to laugh.

"I suppose I'm more angry with myself, for skipping my flight out. Let's hope I make tomorrow's, or I'll most likely be on the post office wanted posters."

"What? Leave without your series on Agamemnon? That's not like you, child. You're too much of a professional for that."

"I also have my quota of good sense."

She sighed and fixed her attention once more on the crude mountain road. How the mammoth old priest had managed to commandeer the canvas-topped army Jeep she was driving was beyond her.

She tugged the white wimple and veil off her head and tossed them into the rear seat. The wind whipped her raven black hair free. "I don't think I'll ask you how you obtained this nun's habit, Father. You might shock my sense of propriety."

"I'm sure the good sister was shocked. Imagine, finding that a thief had violated the sanctuary of St. Agatha's Convent. But comfort yourself, my child; you have managed for the moment to elude Agamemnon's special agents. The VASIK are not noted for their baby-sitting techniques."

"Won't they know where to look for Damon? I'm sure they have files on his place of birth, his employment record, his marriage, things like that."

The priest chuckled. "The Lord works in marvelous ways, my child. When Agamemnon overthrew the monarchy, the university files were burned in one of his staged riots. The general was his own worst enemy."

"But surely Damon had some kind of employment records."

"He was employed by the royal government, I believe, as some kind of an engineer. When he went to work for the PFF his files were deleted from all the computer tapes by a spook the PFF planted in VASIK's security system. I myself took care of the marriage certificate. Legally, Damon Demetrios doesn't exist."

Ahh, but he did. He was all too real for her.

The Jeep sped around a hairpin curve with ease. "How much farther to the village? This habit is about as hot and uncomfortable as a hair shirt."

"By Lady Phillipa's directions, maybe another twenty-five miles," the priest answered. "Just the other side of Lake Niarchos, she said."

The lake, nestled high in the Rhodope Mountains, glistened like a sapphire in the setting sun. Shreds of mist rising off the lake turned the horizon the color of salmon, streaked with ethereal lines of vermillion.

Sigourney didn't know quite what she had expected of Damon's village, but its quaint ambiance soothed the rage that had been seething in her. Stone cottages with thatched roofs dozed lazily against one another. Donkeys grazed on wildflowers pushing up through cracks in the streets of hardened lava, which crossed and recrossed each other without seeming to arrive anywhere.

Somehow she reached the center of the village, a tree-shaded square surrounded on three sides with shops and on the fourth by a traditional Greek Orthodox church. "Damon's home is supposed to be up that street that runs beside the church," Father Murphy told her. "You're to turn off where the street crests the hill."

The "street" was more like an alley, but she found the turnoff easily enough. It meandered for a mile through terraced farmland. The farmhouse, buttressed by gigantic cedars dating back to Charlemagne's rule, might have been a little larger than those in the village, but it was built of the same solid limestone. Rambler roses climbed the walls and a picturesque bridge spanned an idle brook.

She parked the Jeep beside an ox cart. Damon was hunkering by the huge wheel, apparently working on it. Setting aside a wrench, he rose to greet them. He wore a faded-blue chambray shirt with the sleeves rolled halfway up his muscular forearms, and jeans that faithfully followed the strong lines of his hips and thighs.

His shuttered dark blue eyes slid to her before focusing on the priest. "Did anyone try to follow you?"

Father Murphy hefted his bulk out of the Jeep. "I assure you, the hounds of hell couldn't have kept up with this madwoman."

Damon noted her white habit, and his hard mouth eased into a stringent smile. "I see you have come in costume for the festivities tonight."

With rekindled anger—and, yes, excitement—she met his amused glance. "You know why I've come, Damon Demetrios! You set me up!"

"We will talk later. Now I want you and Father Murphy to meet my parents."

A kerosene lamp in the main room was the only defense against the encroaching evening darkness. The floor was of roughly hewn cypress, and the few pieces of furniture were handmade but sturdy. A crucifix and an icon depicting the baptism of Jesus were the only wall decorations.

Damon's mother met them at the kitchen door. She was a tiny, delicate woman, with thick, gray hair bundled atop her head in a careless knot. Her eyes were warm, her smile open and direct, and Sigourney wondered how she had ever produced such a big son as Damon, one so unlike her in looks and personality.

A few minutes later her husband came in from the fields, and the question of Damon's genes was satisfied. He could have been cloned from his father but for the silver that shot through the older man's yellow hair and the fact that his shoulders were slightly bowed from a lifetime in the fields. Both were rugged, possessing a hard male vitality, but Damon's features were stamped with a powerful and ruthless cast.

Neither parent made any comment on the habit she wore, and she could only suppose that with Damon for a son they had learned to accept the unusual.

Sigourney's hand was swallowed up by the older man's handshake. "We welcome you to our home," he said gruffly in stilted English that lacked the warmed-rum quality of Damon's deep voice. "My son has told us of your excellent reputation as a reporter."

Then he reverently bowed his leonine head to the back of the priest's hand, a humble gesture she would have thought uncharacteristic of either father or son. "Your presence blesses our household, Father."

Dinner that evening consisted of chicken baked with tomatoes—and the ubiquitous retsina. When Sigourney passed up the golden wine, Father Murphy teased, "It's not charitable to flaunt your abstemiousness in this way, you know. It merely serves to accentuate my liberal use of unconsecrated wine."

The conversation covered the usual subjects: the weather, crops, local gossip, the festivities later that evening that would wind up the week of Midsummer Midnight. Politics were conspicuously avoided.

Damon's mother's eyes returned again and again to caress her son, as though she were afraid she might not see him again. At the moment, her husband was castigating Damon. "A prodigal son you are! You don't come home often enough. Your sister is almost as bad as you at visiting us."

"Kyros!" his wife admonished. "We are living in a modern age. The young people can't look back and live by the old ways as we did."

"Bah, woman! Our son has not forgotten respect for tradition." For all his fearsome glare, the old man surprised Sigourney by gently, surreptitiously, holding his wife's hand, even as he continued to rant.

Sigourney looked at Damon. With an expression of mild amusement, he listened to his father. The father caught the glimmer in his son's eyes and startled everyone by delivering a shout of laughter. "Ha! I am a foolish old man!" His hand slapped the table. "Come, we go to the festivities!"

Damon's mother knotted a woolen head scarf under her chin against the cool mountain night, and her husband donned a pair of wooden shoes and a homespun tunic. Damon briefly inspected Sigourney's religious vestment and asked, "Where is your luggage?"

"Lady Phillipa said she would have it stored for me in a locker at airport customs." She watched Damon closely, but his expression didn't even flicker at the mention of the woman's name.

"I will see that you get some proper clothing. For now..." His dark gaze slid once more over the long, white habit that contrasted with the ebony length of hair mantling her shoulders. "For now what you're wearing will do."

They all walked the mile down to the village plaza, where costumed dancers whirled by the light of paper lanterns to the bouzouki, balalaika and tambourine. The men wore short full-skirted costumes with long white woolen tights and heavily braided jackets. The laughing women looked almost like gypsies in their long, brightly colored skirts and full-sleeved white blouses, with golden bangles hanging around their necks. On the far side of the plaza a fireswallower entertained wide-eyed children, and a stooped old woman sold garlands of oleanders.

When the dancers stopped, the traditional *syrtos* began its repetitious and relentless melody. The townspeople hurried to form circles, and Sigourney found herself drawn toward one of the circles with Damon. Uncertain, she looked to him, and he dipped his head to her ear, saying, "Watch the others and follow them."

She kicked off her heels, which were inappropriate for a nun anyway, and stepped in line next to Damon. Slowly the circle of dancers began to rotate, first in one direction, then the other, in what seemed nothing but a shuffling gait. However, as the tempo of the music increased, so did the rhythm of the steps. Holding the hand of a middle-aged woman on one side and Damon's on the other, she kept her eyes on him, following his movements. For such a large man, he moved with a fluid grace.

She laughed, trying to keep up with the rapid kicking, pirouetting, squatting, and slapping of hands sharply on the thighs. Her habit swirled about her legs, and she imagined that she had never looked less a nun than at that moment, dancing in her bare feet, her touseled hair fanning down to her waist.

As the music crescendoed and ended, she collapsed against Damon's chest, breathless and laughing. "Oh, my aching thighs," she gasped. "And my deflated lungs!"

"It is the altitude," he said.

He had braced supporting hands about her ribs, and when she looked up to meet his smoldering glance she felt what was becoming a familiar shock of excitement. Shudders rocked her body. "It's not the altitude, it's the cigarettes," she murmured inanely.

Abruptly he released her waist and grasped her upper arm. "A cigarette is not such a bad idea right now. I believe you wanted to talk?"

Without waiting for her answer, he picked up her high heels and led her through the maze of merrymakers and up an alley crowded with shops closed for the celebration. In a darkened shop doorway, a young couple embraced passionately. She studiously averted her eyes and concentrated instead on the steep, winding pathway.

When the shops and houses had dwindled to only a few, Damon lit a cigarette and passed it to her, then lit one for himself as they continued walking.

"An American brand," she said accusingly. "You didn't change brands, did you? You knew I would be coming tonight, just as you knew I would go with you to Rhodes."

He didn't answer, and she kept walking, matching her stride to his longer one. Her anger continued to build. "You manipulate people, Damon," she said at last, not bothering to look at him. "It's remarkable, that callous mind of yours." She inhaled deeply, bitterly, on the cigarette. "You plot the course, and no matter what the cost, you carry on, even if it means the death of young people who hardly know what they're fighting for!"

"I have been lectured and chastised and insulted many times, Sigourney, and it does not bother me."

"My God, Damon! You don't need to be a military dictator or a Nazi to become a murderer. Can't you understand that people can kill just as well in the name of democracy or freedom or Christianity as they did in the name of the Third Reich?''

He halted on an outcropping of rock and flipped his cigarette into the night. Below, the village lights shimmered through interlaced tree branches. In the moonlight his handsome face was as hard and cold as marble. "Appeasement never works, Sigourney. It did not with Hitler, and it will not with Agamemnon.''

"Damon, just what do you want of me?''

He rose and faced her. His expression was dark, enigmatic. "I want you to cover the approaching revolution.''

"Find someone else!'', she snapped. "I'm not interested in documenting the bloodthirsty madness of a war.''

"I do not want your stock-in-trade answer,'' he shot back. "I have already read it in the interview in *World Report*." His hands grasped her shoulders, holding her immobile, but his voice was patient. "Sigourney, I think it is time you talked about the past. About your childhood.''

She could feel tremors stirring in the pit of her stomach, like shockwaves before an earthquake. If she didn't get hold of herself immediately, she wouldn't be able to stop her shaking.

With a gentle joggle of her shoulders, he said, "I want to know. I have a feeling even Father Murphy does not know everything.''

Half a dozen times she tried to speak, but she accomplished only short, unconnected whispers. The years of terror were locked deeply inside her. Damon pulled her close. His large hand on the back of her head pressed her cheek against his chest. "Talk."

A flood of unpleasant memories beat at the carefully erected dam. Damon's tender coaxing was cracking the dam. To share the horror of those memories was terribly tempting. "My father..."

She halted, trying to find the words to speak objectively, words that didn't reach down too close to the gut pain level, and started again.

"My father was an American GI. After the United States withdrew its troops from Korea, my father remained. He became a local resistance fighter against Communist infiltration, and my mother and I didn't see much of him. Actually, I don't have many memories of either of my parents, Damon. I remember when I was about five, my mother died from God-knows-what disease—and my father, well, he simply failed to return one day."

She was proud of herself; she had related her childhood, matter-of-factly and in a tidy summary without losing her self-imposed control.

"His leaving hurt you, did it not?"

She tilted her head back to stare at Damon. In his eyes she read the compassion that could be her downfall. Or was this tender side of him only another aspect of the calculating man she knew he could be?

"Shall I tell you the more gruesome details of my childhood?" she bit out in a self-preserving instinct to separate herself from the gentle danger of this man. "Shall I tell you that as a child I slept on the frying-pan pavement outside the Royal Seoul Hotel—that I was dying of starvation and didn't care? Will that convince you that I have no wish to repeat my childhood experiences as an adult? If it doesn't, I have other scenarios that ought to entertain your morbid sense of curiosity."

He kissed her forehead. "Tell me whatever you want." His voice was muffled by her unruly hair.

"Why?" she asked warily, angrily. "Because then you will have a psychological hold on me? Because then I will docilely agree to cover your damned revolution?"

His finger and thumb tilted her chin upward. "Because I want you to understand that until you do involve yourself, you will always be running away from your past and from your fears."

Overhead the stars were being extinguished by the rapidly brightening dawn. "Damn you, Damon," she whispered.

Chapter 7

After Sigourney had hung the public telephone receiver on its hook, her drachma clattered into the coin return assembly. She collected the coin and made her way across the cracked and oil-stained concrete wharf to the Jeep. She was oblivious to the appreciative whistles from the nearby Balkan shipyards, where workers were overhauling a three-story-high ship's propeller amidst a maze of equipment and scaffolding.

A fisherman's billed cap concealed her wealth of jet black hair, but the jeans and lavender T-shirt she had bought in the bustling Macedonian seaport of Tipraeus testified to lissome curves that could only belong to a female.

"You filed your story?" Father Murphy asked, when she slid behind the steering wheel.

She nodded. "UP agreed to use it. But Agamemnon's already covered himself. He issued a statement this morning that yesterday's attack on the military parade was carried out by Soviet-sponsored terrorists."

For a long moment she sat staring out at the bay. The oil-sheened water was a clutter of shipping: tankers, fishing dories, cargo vessels, tuna boats, and Macedonian frigates and gunboats. Her nostrils flared reflexively at the briny tang of the sea.

At last she said, "I have to be out of my mind, Father. Here I am, traipsing after a freedom fighter in the name of journalism. Being a roving war correspondent was never my thing."

He studied her sympathetically, his craggy features softening. "You're in love with Damon Demetrios, aren't you?"

She tossed her chin in a scoffing gesture. "For a priest, you have a lot of romantic notions."

"Listening to confessions gives a priest a lot of insight."

"But as a priest you don't realize that a man can be very attractive to a woman, especially an older woman like myself, without there being the least bit of seriousness attached to it." She started the engine. "I like and admire Damon very much, but that's all there is to it."

"Damon isn't just any man."

Her blue eyes darkened. "That's just the problem." She swung the Jeep away from the docks and headed toward the coastal highway. "Damon is one of those mythological gods descended from Mount Olympus, superheroes who don't need anyone, especially mere mortals."

"There you are wrong. I think he needs you, Sigourney. I've seen it in his eyes in unguarded moments."

Her lips eased into a sad smile. "In your saintly naivete, Father, you have mistaken lust for need."

She reached their destination shortly before sundown, as instructed by Damon. The boat waiting in the cypress-concealed cove was larger than the yawl. Like a ghost ship, it lay silently at anchor beneath a canopy of green leaves. It looked abandoned. The screech of forest birds was the only indication of life.

She got out of the Jeep and handed the keys to the priest. "Are you certain it's another shipment of bibles you're going to pick up at the border?"

The priest's face screwed up in indignation. "I would never commit the sin of lying, my child." The rubbery lips stretched into an apologetic grin. "Perhaps, though, the sin of omission. I may have failed to add that the bibles have been hollowed out to hold medical supplies."

"My, my. To what depths of depravity will you sink next, Father?"

Watching him drive off, she understood why he preferred her at the wheel of the Jeep. The four-wheel drive vehicle lurched, sputtered, swerved, then seemed to steady itself before it leaped forward out of sight.

At the forested shore, she knelt to roll up her jeans. She was stalling, mentally preparing herself, before she waded out to the trawler—and Damon.

Anticipation and a certain fear ran through her like a roller coaster. She was already tired of the physical drain that she underwent whenever she was in his presence, and she was actually a little frightened of the power of his land, whose history was as old as the sea and sunlight and civilization itself. She longed to return to her normal routine. Anything was better than this uncertainty.

Why *was* she doing this? If the VASIK tracked her down, she wouldn't be dealt with gently. The thought of the notorious Toridallos Military Prison sent a chain re-action of shudders through her body and made her palms damp.

On the other hand, the professional side of her ac-cepted Damon's challenge. An in-depth series on the Macedonian revolution could still earn her the Pulitzer Prize she coveted.

Yet it was more than that. She was going to beat Da-mon at his own game, on his own turf. Nevertheless, her recklessness frightened her. She knew she was afraid of him. He could defeat her.

Suddenly he loomed up before her, appearing in the shadow of the trees like a dark and forbidding force. The sound of his coming was muffled by the breaking of the surf against the shore. She stared up at him, bemused.

He showed almost no effects of having gone without sleep the night before. He had left on some mission after their return to the farmhouse, and she had slept in the bed he had been using. Consequently she spent a restless night, pounding the pillow, turning from one side to the other, while his masculine scent insidiously permeated her senses and her very pores.

He wore jeans and a brown windbreaker. A man's slicker was slung over his shoulder, and he handed it to her. "It may rain before we get there."

She stood up and shook back the hair that had fallen over one shoulder. "Thank you." She gestured at the duffel bag of reporter's paraphernalia at her feet. "I'm ready."

He took a step closer, and his eyes probed her upturned face. "You are sorry you agreed to come?"

Sigourney didn't want him to come any nearer. In that virgin forest they were alone, as alone as the first man and woman, and her psychological defenses were being terribly battered.

"Yes, I am," she said softly.

"I could let you return. But I need you."

"You need my help," she qualified.

"You are a terribly complicated woman, Sigourney."

She picked up her duffel bag. "The sun has set. Shall we go aboard?"

This trawler was old and rotted and reeked of dead fish—sardines, which she had never been able to stomach. Breathing shallowly, she stepped carefully around a pile of fishing nets and ancient hemp ropes. Damon revved up the engine. It purred quietly, telling her that it had been refitted for something other than fishing.

"You use this for gun running?" she asked.

It was too dark to see his face. "When we can get the guns."

"Just where are you taking me?"

"One of the wooded islands off the coast. From time to time we move the PFF training camp out among the islands. We should reach the place just before midnight."

She settled back against the wooden hull and assumed her safe role as interviewer. "Tell me, once you decided to form this 'army of self-defense,' how did you go about it?"

He stood at the wheel, silent for a moment, and she knew he was deciding what and what not to tell her. "Certain leaders of the Macedonian Provisional Army contacted me first. To agree to their methods...knowing that innocent women and children would be hurt...

"Anyway, there were other people who felt as I did. We decided to arm ourselves quietly and train a militia in secret. This armed force would be used for one purpose and one purpose alone: defense. The official agencies of both the MPA and the New Democracy Party disclaim all knowledge of our force publicly, and privately cooperate with its growth and activities."

She had to admire his audacity and his bravery. She worried secretly that he might discover just how really spineless she was. If he had begun to appreciate what she was doing, his respect could vanish in an instant.

A misty sprinkle began, but he didn't seem to notice. She disdained the bulky raincoat, and rather than seek shelter below the control console, she stayed at Damon's side. She wanted to hear his voice, the reassurance of it, its low, vibrant timbre.

With raindrops caressing her face and plastering her hair to her neck and shoulders, she felt an exhilaration one could only experience outside the realm of day-to-day existence. Lids closed, she tilted her face upward. What was it Damon had told her? "When the danger was over and nothing had happened to you, you felt twice alive"? She suspected that with Damon the danger was never over.

She looked at his strong profile. "Why do you do it, Damon? Why do you choose to live the hunted life of a criminal?"

"You might as well ask the same of men who live wherever freedom is in jeopardy. The Lech Walesas of the world. There are thousands of them. You will find them in Poland, Israel, Northern Ireland, Central America."

"But I'm asking *you*."

He cut back the throttle a little, apparently centering his attention on guiding the boat. With the rain *ping*ing off the deck, she wasn't certain he had heard her. At last he spoke.

"Eleven years ago I was a civil engineer with the Department of the Interior. You might say we were building a better Macedonia. Bridges, dams, highways—the airport you flew into. Trying to upgrade a third-world country and adopt the modern technology of the industrial nations. Agamemnon's coup put a halt to that."

"But why you, Damon? Why not let someone else risk their life?"

"Why anyone? Why does there have to be such—" He broke off with a snarl of frustration and ran a hand through the damp mass of his wild, golden curls.

She wanted to reach out and touch the muscle that jerked spasmodically in his jaw.

"As I told you," he said, his normally dispassionate voice taut with tension, "I do not trust words that much. But I will finish answering your question; the subject will not be raised again."

Suddenly she didn't want to know anything about his past. It would be a tie to bind her. "It's stopped raining," she said, hoping to distract him.

He didn't seem to hear her. "After the coup, the law became the gun held in the hands of a soldier—often undisciplined, illiterate and sometimes drunk. Later, five, six months after the takeover, maybe more, my wife and daughter..."

She could hear the terrible anguish in his voice, and she wanted to plead with him to stop. Her own agony writhed inside her as he continued, his sentences fragmented.

"They were traveling by bus to my wife's hometown...her parents' anniversary.... Agamemnon's soldiers, one of his killer squads that roved the country—they stopped the bus...accused certain people on it of being antinational...just arbitrarily hauled them off and shot them in front of the rest of the passengers...in front of my daughter."

"Your wife," she choked. "She was one of the people they executed?"

Either he didn't hear her or he chose not to acknowledge her question. His mouth was stretched in a ghastly grimace, like a gargoyle's. "I learned later from one of the passengers that a couple of soldiers took my daughter with them. My God, she was so young. A child, really. When Irinia's body was found—ironic that my wife should choose the name 'Irinia' for our daughter…it meant, *means*, 'peace'—Irinia had been raped. I don't know how many times."

"Oh, my God."

Sigourney didn't know what else to say. She, who had such a command of words, felt totally inadequate at that moment. Her eyes were soft and compassionate, and she wanted to enfold Damon in her arms.

Worse, she wanted to become his lover again, to know the rapture of being held in those mighty arms. After a long interval, she said softly, "You've let no one in your life since then, have you?"

"There's no room in my life for anything else."

At first the island was a mere dot, slightly darker than the night surrounding it. As the trawler drew nearer to the coastline, Damon flashed the boat's spotlight in a prearranged code that was answered by a light from ashore. By the time the boat docked, four shadowy figures were waiting on the pier.

"Give me your hand," Damon said, helping her from the trawler to the flimsy dock.

Only when a high-powered fluorescent lantern was held aloft was she able to distinguish faces and figures.

Dressed in camouflage fatigues, the three men had superb physiques.

The lone woman's angular figure made a mockery of Sigourney's soft contours. As the young girl inspected Sigourney, her expression clouded over. Hers was the face of the Romany wanderers: full, carmine lips; flat cheekbones; the midnight black eyes. Her straight hair, a shade of brown that was difficult to distinguish in the false light of the lantern, was cut just below the jaw in a severe style that flattered her square face.

Damon introduced her only as Melina, then quickly named off the other three.

The man who seemed to be in charge, Major Veronos, shook Sigourney's hand. His features were nondescript. He was the sort of man the FBI or CIA might employ, one who would pass unnoticed in a crowd of people. But Veronos had sharp eyes set in his regular features. His welcoming smile was reserved.

"You are sure you know what you are doing, coming here, Miss Hamilton?" The question might have been meant for her, but Veronos's glance was directed at Damon. "You take a great chance in doing this."

"I think what you mean, Major, is that Damon is taking a great chance in bringing me, isn't it? The question is whether I can be trusted or not. Am I correct?"

"You are perceptive. Yes, Damon is taking a risk, but I have complete faith in his judgment."

Melina's clipped voice interrupted. "Has Damon warned you that should you be caught in a raid on the training center, you face certain imprisonment—or worse? I have been told you are an American. I do not think you American women have any concept of hardship, or what it means to live under the constant threat of danger.''

Sigourney lifted a brow at the girl's blunt antagonism. It could have been simply a female soldier's contempt for a woman who has assumed a more common feminine role—or it could have been the reaction of a woman in love who senses a challenger, competition for the man she loves.

Impatience curbed Damon's voice. ''The light could attract notice. Let us get on to camp.''

Camp was certainly not the well-fortified shelter of the kibbutzim Sigourney had toured with Golda Meir in Israel. The barbed-wire fence that surrounded the compound deep in the pine forest could easily have been breached; the guards who saluted the major and Damon looked exhausted.

She passed dozens of tents, but few soldiers slept inside, because of the steamy heat. Along with the rest of the major's entourage, she picked her way among the scores of men and women sleeping in bedrolls on the hard ground, dampened by the recent rain. The ragtag commandoes were too tired to awaken at their approach. A few of them slept with rifles at their sides.

Major Veronos led them to a barnlike building that did duty as headquarters, supply room, laundry and mess hall. Raw plasterboard partitioned the inside into cubicles. The primitive building's few windows, all positioned high on the walls, were spray-painted black.

The major directed the group to a table at the rear of the mess hall and sent one of the soldiers—a freckle-faced youth who could have been no more than seventeen or eighteen—to the kitchen for coffee for everyone. Melina slid onto the bench next to Damon.

The major offered Sigourney a cigarette, and as he lit it for her, she listened to Melina telling Damon what had transpired in his absence. "We have found a way, Damon, to make delayed explosives out of—"

Sigourney didn't catch the rest, but it was apparent that the young woman was eager to claim his attention. As an observer of people and their habits, Sigourney noted the slight tension in the way the girl held her head, the awkward pauses in her small talk. The young woman was obviously in love.

"As you can see, Miss Hamilton," the major was saying, "we don't have adequate facilities for training recruits." Had he purposely diverted her attention from the other conversation? "Israel has been fortunate enough to be able to depend on contributions from sympathetic Americans, as Northern Ireland has depended on Irish-American organizations in the States."

"Just what kind of instruction goes on here?"

"Our training is a rigorous program of basic military and physical fitness courses lasting four to six weeks. Into this period we cram lessons in unarmed combat, training in weapons, field craft, elementary Morse Code, radio transmission, map reading and unconventional warfare. There are frequent all-night exercises. Basically it amounts to instruction in resistance. Passive resistance. We learn to subdue, not to kill, Miss Hamilton.''

''I heard talk just now of detonations and explosives. They kill, Major.''

''Not necessarily. They can be used to wipe out radar installations, military supplies, computer terminals. Sabotage. Anything to hinder and disrupt the work of Agamemnon's government. What you'll write about one day in the near future will not be a little war of snipers and hit-and-run tactics and guerrilla warfare. It will be an all-out revolution.''

The freckle-faced soldier came back with a tray of coffee cups, and Sigourney stubbed out her cigarette. For once she found her coffee watery. Didn't the Macedonians know a happy medium in making coffee?

''You must understand about my articles, Major; they'll deal more with personalities than ideals. I'm not trying to be arbitrary. I just write best from that aspect, and that's what you want from me—the best coverage I can give. Right?''

''You are a difficult woman, Miss Hamilton.''

She slid a glance at Damon, who was watching her through the haze of pungent cigarette smoke. ''I've recently been called a complicated woman, Major. I suppose 'difficult' is no worse.''

''You will need to be more than difficult to survive this training,'' Melina told her, her sloe eyes flashing.

Damon flicked the girl a silencing look, and said to Sigourney, ''The recruits here learn self-confidence. That self-confidence grows into a sense of physical power and superiority that few men—or women—ever acquire. By the time they finish our training, the graduates will willingly tackle any man, whatever his strength, size or ability. They learn to face the possibility of a fight without the slightest tremor of apprehension, a state of mind which very few professional boxers ever enjoy and which so often means more than half the battle."

Sigourney lifted an eyebrow. "Is this the pep talk you saved to convert me to the PFF cause?"

"I do not think you would make it through commando training," Melina interrupted with a sneer.

"I don't think I would want to," she snapped back. "Administering pain is not one of my specialties."

Damon's eyes glinted with what she suspected was amusement, which irked her inexplicably.

"Physical defense is not all that is stressed here," Major Veronos said. "PFF training includes a course in clandestine tactics and security. The recruits learn the importance of looking natural and ordinary while doing unnatural and extraordinary things. They learn how to shadow someone and keep them under surveillance; how to avoid surveillance; how to locate a safe house and when to change addresses; how to adopt simple but effective disguises; and how to keep a cover. They learn the use of passwords, codes and ciphers, and we even have an ex-burglar who teaches lock picking and safe-breaking."

"Sounds delightful," she murmured dryly.

When they had finished the coffee, Damon showed her the supply room, where he requisitioned sleeping bags for them from the female clerk. The strong smell of lye soap drifted from the laundry room next door, where a hamper of soiled clothes blocked the doorway.

Outside, she looked around her, trying to decide just where to roll out her sleeping bag. "I think it is best, under the circumstances, if you stay with me," Damon said, standing at her side. "An early rising recruit might feel that you are fair game."

"I assumed that this place was run with the strict discipline of an army post," she said, following him into the darkness.

"Our soldiers are not conscripted. They are volunteers. Men and women who must somehow make some kind of normalcy of their interrupted lives."

"You seem to be adept at taking my remarks and turning them around to make them sound prudish," she told him, feeling a little put out.

He stopped and looked at her. "Must the two of us always be so defensive with each other, Sigourney?"

She refused to look away from his unrelenting stare. "I suppose I'm merely tired," she hedged.

He rolled out his sleeping bag in a deserted area that she assumed was used for target practice. Hay bales stretched in rows across a large clearing. The musty odor of straw mingled with the fragrance of pine needles freshened by the rain. The moon darted in and out of wisps of scurrying black clouds, and a lone cricket chirped a song of tribute to the night's beauty.

She waited silently as Damon took her sleeping bag from her and shook it out several feet away from his.

When he had finished, he sat back on his haunches and looked up at her. "You are afraid of me."

She forced herself to slide into the sleeping bag while he held it open for her. He hunkered over her, his face a dark blur. In her ears she could hear the pounding of her pulse, an echo of the distant thunder. "Yes, I am," she admitted after a long, painful moment.

"Why? Tell me."

"Because the relationship you would like—"

"The relationship I would like is not hypocritical. I want you. Have I not made it plain?"

"I don't go to bed with a man merely because of a strong sexual urge," she fired back.

"Why would you go to bed with a man?" he snapped.

"Because I cared deeply for him and wanted to share more with him than just a noble cause." She took a deep breath and added, "And because I would know he cared for and needed me."

"Sigourney, I want to do all the things that a man and woman do in the United States. But this isn't the United States. There is no time here for the niceties of a romantic attachment."

She could feel the beginnings of a headache. "I expect only that our relationship continue as it has."

"You're an intelligent woman, Sigourney. Do you sincerely think it can?"

"As long as I feel the way I do—yes."

"And what way is that?"

She looked away, unable to withstand the intensity of his gaze. "Disgust at myself for caring about you," she said baldly.

"I do not understand a woman like you."

"Sometimes I don't understand myself, if that's any consolation. But I will tell you this, Damon. You spoke once of making love. You don't know what love is. You're a warlord, incapable of feeling. The Greek warrior," she jeered softly. "I want you to know I intend to walk away from this revolution with a Pulitzer Prize story—and when I do, I intend to forget you."

She rolled onto her far side and snapped, "Good night, Damon."

Chapter 8

Beneath the hot noonday sun Sigourney listened to the martial arts instructions. "What you will learn," Damon told the thirty-odd recruits encircling him, "will be a mixture of jujitsu, karate and what might be termed scientific barroom brawling"—a remark that brought an immediate ripple of nervous laughter.

Damon permitted a brief, cold smile to flash across his face before he went on. "You will be taught to punch not as a boxer punches, which could fracture the knuckles, but with the heel or the edge of the hand, or with extended fingers against the sensitive and vulnerable parts of the enemy's body."

Later, she watched him demonstrate resistance to attack, watched him feign driving a fist into the fleshy region just below a volunteer's solar plexus and then shove the man's chin into his raised knee. He showed how to drive the heel of the hand up under the bridge of a man's nose and how to protect the genitals, how to duck the chin to the chest and whip the body to the side in one fluid motion.

In amazement, she listened as he went on to dispassionately explain how to push a man's eyes out like grapes popping from their skins. Was this the same man who had played with Sotoris's daughters, who had consoled her after her nightmare?

Eleven years had passed since the deaths of his wife and daughter. How much of his capacity to love had been burned from his soul? Damon's sensitivity to her feelings was extraordinary, but he held his response to those feelings in tight check. How could he ever love her? Against the on-going tragedy of the war, her feelings were insignificant. Who was she to question this man's abruptness, his remoteness, his single-minded dedication to a cause of which she wanted no part?

She tried to remind herself that he was a political outlaw, that whatever went on inside his head was alien to her way of thinking. He was the product of his past, as she was of hers.

Yet a part of her identified the other half of herself in him. He would fill the internal cavities that for the span of her life had waited for something unperceived. Being with him would be a union more intricate and perilous than she believed she had the courage to face.

Lunch was a repetition of breakfast's hard bread, handful of olives and watery coffee. Damon was closeted with Major Veronos, and she busied herself with interviewing some of the inductees. Many of them were young, having graduated from youth-organization training to these commando tactics as easily as an ROTC student graduating to army boot camp. The stories they told her were ones she had known intimately. Tales of imprisonment, torture and death. Their stories reeked with fear, hate, sadness, and sometimes all three.

In another area, recruits hurled oranges instead of hand grenades and drilled with brooms instead of automatic rifles. Everything was in short supply—weapons, ammunition, medicine, food, temper.

An older woman with flaming red hair streaked with gray zealously lectured the dozen recruits grouped around her. "You hold in your hand a weapon. Never use it in anger or revenge. Only for defense."

Sigourney made notes, questioned the trainees, watched and listened. Later that afternoon she talked with Melina. Or tried to. As they walked out to the gunnery range, the young woman looked at her as if she despised her—and sometimes with a yearning that said Sigourney was everything she wanted to be.

"How could you possibly understand what we feel?" Melina demanded as they toured the makeshift gunnery. "You are rich and well born."

Sigourney made no attempt to contradict her, but let her rave on. "You do not know the privilege it is just to wake up each morning. You do not know how it feels to fire a rifle until it is too hot to hold."

The girl stopped midway in her harangue to berate an acne-pitted soldier. He had discharged a useless shot at the moving bull's-eye that slid along a horizontal line behind a platform of simulated tree trunks. "Do not shoot unless your bullet has a clear target. You cannot afford to waste ammunition!"

Sigourney spent three more days at the training center. Each night she slept on the hard ground next to Damon, but even when she awoke at dawn, he was gone. What had awakened her? The simple but pressing need to see him each morning? Later in the day she would come upon him in one of the headquarters offices poring over a topographic map or scrawling notations on a pad, a cup of cold, watery coffee untouched before him.

One evening at supper, when they had been on the island four days, Damon told her that they would be leaving at dawn. She was almost sorry to leave, because for that little time she had felt an integral part of what he was about, and thus a part of him.

"Where do we go from here?" she asked with feigned indifference as she nibbled on olives, which she was growing heartily sick of eating. She was considering raiding the crates of bruised oranges reserved for hand grenade practice.

"On an archeological dig," he answered, a challenging smile exposing his strong teeth.

"I knew I shouldn't have asked," she shot back.

When dawn broke she was on the trawler with him, heading back to the mainland, where an empty car, a different one this time, awaited them. She had had little sleep over the past few days, and dark smudges ringed her eyes, but he seemed fresh, prepared for the day ahead.

After several hours of driving they arrived at a dusty pit outside the ancient marketplace of Melpomene, overlooking the valley of Alexandros, Macedonia's main military training center.

In the excavation, pickmen half squatted, elbows braced on knees, and swung their implements from side to side, skimming off thin layers of soil. Now and again a digger paused to feel the earth and then tossed an object into his basket. In another area a second grid of heavy-duty string was being staked out, looking to Sigourney's uneducated eye like a giant waffle.

A tall, leathery, scarecrow of an American climbed out of the pit to greet them with a hearty handshake. Dr. Malcolm held up a human bone and said, "Can you imagine—twenty-five hundred years old and this well preserved! This soil's rich enough to make a stick bloom!"

As they walked over to a house trailer on the site, the archeologist talked about the dig. Inside, a laboratory had been set up, presumably for further detective work on the artifacts. Cigar boxes filled with pottery shards and bits of bones littered the counter. A box of compartmentalized trays sat next to a compact refrigerator, along with a drying screen.

Dr. Malcolm picked up the screen and lifted its secret bottom to expose a tray which held several photographs. He passed one to Damon. "This is an infrared photo of Alexandros at night, Damon—look there, see the shadowy line. That's three new TM-71 tanks rolling out of a moving van from Albania.''

"When did the van arrive?"

"Two days ago. And there's more. Look at this one. That's a Soviet-built tank, or I'm not an archeologist. Obviously, Agamemnon knows resistance is building and is preparing accordingly.''

Sigourney left the two and went outside, feeling a great weariness. She was tired of the constant physical exhaustion. She was tired of being afraid. She was tired of walking that fine line with Damon, of pretending indifference, of feigning courage, of being acutely aware of his every movement. Her nerves were strung as tightly as the grid wires at the dig.

"There is an apartment in Old Town," he told her on the return drive into Constantine. "I use it sometimes as a base. You can use it to get some sleep while I am gone. I have another contact I need to meet.''

Just that. A contact to meet. No other information about where he was going, whom he was meeting, when he would return. Could she live from day to day like that, never knowing, just waiting?

Sigourney prowled the small, bare apartment that would have been razed long ago in any American community. The tiny rooms over a leather shop were like many of the apartments lost in the meandering backstreets of Old Town. The smells of the area were foreign to her, its sounds loud and distracting.

The day was hot, and she couldn't sleep. She worried that Damon might not return. Agamemnon's agents could pick up his trail, could ambush him. What if they marred his beautiful face or hurt him in other ways?...What if she never saw him again?!

Damon seemed indestructible, but he took risks no other man did because he had absolutely nothing to lose. He had suffered the annihilation of his family and survived solitary confinement at Toridallos. He had no anxiety about what could happen to himself. He was fearless and foolhardy at the same time. He allowed himself no personal ties. His dedication to a free Macedonia was enough for him; it kept him above and beyond human emotions.

She looked around the apartment; there was little of Damon to personalize it. A disposable razor and a can of shaving foam in a bathroom that sported an old-fashioned pull-chain toilet. A coffee-stained cup in the kitchen's cracked porcelain sink. Half a liter of curdled milk in a refrigerator that labored like an asthmatic patient. Rumpled sheets that no longer bore the imprint of his magnificent body. *Damon. Damon. Damon.* His name was a pulsing rhythm in her mind. Every breath she took was an echo of his name, thundering in her brain and throbbing in her veins. She knew now that she had simply been marking time until the night he slipped into the taxi and took possession of her waking thoughts and dream-haunted sleep.

Evening shadows spilled through the slatted window shutters when Damon finally filled the apartment's doorway. With a small cry she ran to him and threw her arms about his neck. He pressed her head against his chest, and she could feel his pulse beating strong.

His big hand stroked her hair. "What is it?" he asked gently.

"I was afraid," she mumbled against his shirt. "Afraid you wouldn't return."

"You have been very brave, Sigourney."

His talk of bravery was obviously the closest he could come to giving something of himself to her. She hugged the praise to her as a form of a declaration of love and would not let herself consider the possibility that she might be deceiving herself.

She lifted her head, lips parted, eyes glistening with tears of relief. "Damon, for as much time as we have together, I want to be here, where you are. I want to know your lovemaking. I want to become a part of you in the only way I may ever be able to."

His eyes searched her face for a long moment. "You are sure?"

She nodded.

His fingers tunneled through her mass of hair and tilted her head back. Beneath his impassioned gaze, her eyes closed. His mouth ravaged hers, and she knew that he, too, had been holding back, suppressing his desire for her, waiting. The power of her need washed through her.

"Sigourney. Sigourney."

The way he said her name, fiercely, hungrily, made her body quiver as if it had been hit by lightning. She needed his love now, though she knew it could vanish as quickly as a dandelion puffed by the wind.

He bent to scoop her into his arms and cradle her against his chest. Carrying her as effortlessly as he might an automatic rifle, he strode across the room to the bed. When he lowered her to the mattress, she didn't want to let go, but his hands left her waist only to begin disrobing her. Her blouse and trousers were discarded at the foot of the bed, along with her undergarments.

When she lay naked before him, a peripheral part of her mind wondered if he found her beautiful. But even that thought was fleeting. She had waited too long for him. All of her life. She wanted to feel his heaviness atop her. She wanted him buried deep inside her.

At last he too was naked, the patch of golden hair on the front of his body arrowing toward the magnificence of his loins. For a minute they just held each other, not wanting to move too quickly, to lose their heat. She felt like a shy adolescent virgin.

He leaned over to possess her mouth, his tongue sweeping inside. She pulled him closer, wanting him to crush the aching need from her, and brushed her breasts back and forth against his chest, shivering. She had forgotten their need to be touched.

At first they groped delicately at each other, looking, touching, a feather-light kiss on the shoulder, cheeks grazing. Then, when she felt engorged, as if her inner self could burst through, he raised his knee against her secret flesh and she let out a little moan of pleasure. She forgot about her love for him, forgot about everything but the whirlpool of desire sucking her downward.

She wanted to know the violence of his passion as well as its tenderness. She lashed her tongue along his chest and closed her teeth on his small, hard nipples. Once again she was starving, but this time for him. She would never be able to get enough of him. He brought his hand under her back and pulled it quickly past her buttocks, then down along the insides of her thighs, spreading them.

"Yes," she said. "Now."

He lowered himself onto her and pressed her breasts flat beneath his immense weight. He took hold of the dream behind her eyes and inhabited it. She could sense his deliberate restraint at the center of her madness. She offered herself up to him. Easily, he was inside her, and her head lifted sightlessly, finding his waiting mouth to lose herself in her fantasy.

She kissed his muscle-corded neck, pressed her fingers into the hollows beneath his shoulder blades, moved her hips in undulation with his thrusts. Even as she did, she was keenly aware of him, of his masculine smell, of his delicate eyelids, of the faint down that ridged his ears. Her love for him was a living thing.

She was making love to him, and she discovered in doing so a frightful combination of pain and pleasure, of reality and illusion. This fusion of flesh was the only answer to life's pain.

Their mating was a metaphysical melting and fitting, a pure and violent soldering. Egos were laid aside. The emptiness that she had carried was being filled to overbrimming. She was lost. Vainly, she tried to keep the moment in sight; she wanted to know this love forever, exactly as she did at that fleeting moment. There was a tremendous humming in her ears that was more than the singing of her blood. Then she felt the explosion of air from her lungs.

She reached the peak too quickly. Behind her lids she knew that the blank, ordered harmony of her existence was altered irrevocably.

When she opened her eyes, he was watching her with a look she could not identify. Embarrassment flushed her skin. "Thank you," she said, hearing the stiltedness in her voice. He had not found release in her, and it was like a slap in the face.

His hand caressed her cheek and smoothed the length of her inky hair over the mattress's edge. "Sigourney, can you understand...can you understand that what you want from me existed only before Agamemnon overthrew the government?"

Something like shrapnel exploded in her brain. "I'm not begging for your love, damn you, Damon!" Her voice was a low whiplash. "I wanted only to give. Are you so proud, so arrogant, that you can't accept even that much?"

"I do not want you to be hurt."

The words were a muttering on the lips that crushed hers ruthlessly. He drove into her then with a frenzy, whispering her name over and over as if it were a means to hold back the storm of which they were the center, the hurricane's eye.

She could feel building in him the need to have what he had been too long denied. He twisted so she was shifted atop him, his big hands supporting her back, and she rode him, sobbing for the fleeting, exquisite moment that would soon be lost to her.

"Sigourney, Sigourney, I am so close right now." His breathing was ragged, and he was trembling, sweat trickled from his temples. For this one moment he was hers.

The rhythm of moving in unison with him, giving, accepting, taking, holding, propelled her higher, higher, higher, to an unsustainable plateau of pleasure, a rhapsody of sensation. Then they found release together, in what for her was a moment of sharp, pure ecstasy, a moment that she sensed would be followed by an infinity of yearning for what had been so quickly lost.

The days blurred from one to another in an idyllic progression. The tiny apartment with its cracked walls and peeling paint became for her a place of sheer beauty. It shut out the interference of a strife-ridden world, made reality out of her fantasy. Within those four walls she came to know the exquisite joy of sex when it was coupled with her deep love for Damon, a love that could not be measured in finite terms, which sometimes frightened her, it was so immense and consuming.

The giving of that love, the total surrendering of her self, threatened to submerge the last shreds of her identity. Still, she gave herself up to the mastery of his hands and afterward to the warmth of his enfolding arms. He was the wildest of men, despite his consummate control, and he could arouse her with words and looks as well as with a touch. She had not known a man could be so gentle, thoughtful and tender, yet so commanding. The tenderness in their lovemaking was something new on his part. It was as if, that second time, they had joined together in passion and cracked a barrier, like the onslaught of the elements that crack a dike holding back a great flood of emotion. Or was she only futilely hoping?

She realized that she was reaching out, trying desperately to touch him over that vast, dark, empty space. And she didn't know if she would succeed. She did know that they had both left detachment behind.

She sensed in Damon an indefinable feeling of softening toward her. At times, times that were all too brief, he permitted her a glimpse of his vulnerability—personal, inconsequential revelations about himself that he would not normally make. Often, while he sat up until dawn at the apartment's wobbly kitchen table, revising a Pan-Hellenic cipher or preparing a brochure that would later be dispersed in Great Britain or the United States, she would sit in a chair, smoking and watching him, storing away the treasured moments to be replayed later. Sometimes she wrote her own dispatches, to be smuggled out by mail or phoned in collect from a public telephone booth.

One afternoon she arranged to meet Father Murphy at a sidewalk cafe within the safe limits of Old Town. The cafe was located in an area that was a maze of booths and shops, reminding her of the *souq* in Tunis.

Its inhabitants never noticed anything out of the ordinary, because everything there was out of the ordinary. Turks in fezzes, Arabs in red tarbooshes, Hassidic Jews in black-brimmed beaver hats and side curls, Greek women in white stockings and aprons—all packed the narrow streets.

Normally she would have had to plan a meeting by night or don her nun's disguise, keeping her head reverently lowered, for her Eurasian features were all too distinguishable. But Agamemnon's VASIK found the old quarter's secrets almost impossible to penetrate. Within the walled section of Constantine thrived a black market and other seamy operations that didn't detract from its exotic appeal; nevertheless, people walked the old, interlacing streets, feeling safer there than they would in any modern metropolis.

Waiting for Father Murphy, she ordered *ouzo*, the anise liqueur, and wistfully watched the young lovers strolling among the crowded booths. They held hands and looked with fulfilled rapture at each other's face.

Their bliss seemed like blasphemy to her, and she shifted her gaze to observe less disquieting things—two boys rolling a metal hoop over the cobblestone pavement, an old woman talking to her caged parakeet, a man in a red beret sketching in charcoal the squirrels that scaled a lone ancient elm.

Seated at a table across from her was a middle-aged man sporting the obligatory camera that labeled him an American. He flirted outrageously with her, even raised his glass in a toast. She was accustomed to stares of admiration and managed a polite smile that implied, "Thank you for the homage, but I'm not interested."

When at last the priest eased his bulk into the wooden folding chair, she turned a brilliant smile on him. "I was afraid you wouldn't make it, Father. These days, my delicate ego couldn't take being stood up in addition to everything else."

"Your ego has never suffered before, my child."

With a wry smile she pushed a large manila envelope of typewritten pages across the table to him. "Can you smuggle these out of Macedonia as easily as you smuggle your bibles in?"

"The Lord works in miraculous ways." As he repeated his favorite phrase, he wedged the envelope beneath his cassock and, when the waiter returned with her *ouzo*, ordered a glass of retsina.

"Father, I have a confession."

"Marvelous, Sigourney. Confession is good for the spirit. It empties the soul and makes room for more sins."

She laughed. "I feel better already, just confessing I have a confession."

His brows beetled down in concern above his sunken eyes, and he leaned forward over the table as far as his girth would permit. "You know I am here to listen, if you need to talk."

She looked down at her drink, and her hair swayed forward to hide her bleak expression, but her fingertip circling the glass's rim betrayed her agitation. "You were right, Father. I am in love with Damon. I...that is, we...have become lovers."

The priest took a sip of the golden wine, then said, "So were Ruth and Boaz. What original kind of sin have you to tell me? Something I haven't heard from others, please. Confessions tend to become unbearably boring with repetition, dear child."

"The sin...I feel no shame for loving him, Father. If it could be within the boundaries of marriage—but it can't." The admission she needed to make was difficult. "The shame I feel, Father...I feel shame only for using that love to beat back the memory of his wife."

She saw no condemnation in the wise old eyes. He said nothing, only waited for her to continue.

"I know that I'll do whatever is necessary to protect him, Father. Damon is brilliant and strong, and as long as there is life in him, there is hope for his love.

"Oh, God!" she cried softly, and put one hand up to shield the pain in her eyes. "Help me. Help me."

The priest's chubby hand closed over the delicate one clenched on the table top. "Your love is strong, Sigourney. If it comes through the test of fire, it can accomplish miracles."

She lowered the other hand from her brow and smiled weakly at him. "You know that adage that adversity builds character, Father?"

"Yes?"

"Well, I want to be shallow."

"Too late for that, my dear." He grinned, his jowls jiggling in response. "I'm afraid that strength of character is inextricably laced all the way through you. You will just have to face the ugly truth."

"If I had any strength of character left, I would leave now. Before it is too late."

"Too late for what?"

She shook her head. "I don't know, Father. I no longer know what I'm saying. I'm not even sure what I'm going to do."

"If you need me to help you in any way, Sigourney, you know I will. You are indeed like my own child. You have been since that moment I found your soulful eyes watching me warily from your domain on the pavement outside the Royal Seoul Hotel."

She stood and dropped some coins on the table to pay for the drinks. "I know that." She shoved a heavy swath of hair back from her forehead in an impatient gesture. "I—I'll let you know."

She turned away, her steps taking her with feverish anticipation back to the little apartment.

Chapter 9

Although Damon was out when Sigourney returned from telephoning in a dispatch dealing with a recent riot outside the National Palace, Lady Phillipa Fleming was waiting. "I'm sorry to keep turning up like a bad penny," she said, "but it's the only way that guarantees security."

"I understand," Sigourney said. "It seemed I ran into an armed soldier on every corner. Martial law is making patriotic feelings run high."

She wanted to be gracious. She liked the woman. Still, Lady Phillipa's presence seemed an intrusion, somehow. Her being there opened the apartment to a world Sigourney had shut out. It forced her to face the jealous question—had the woman ever been here before, with Damon?

His wife had been dead for eleven years now, and it was unrealistic to expect a man like him to remain celibate. It was just as unrealistic to hope that she could ever mean as much to him as his country.

She crossed to the refrigerator. "Could I offer you a glass of wine? Amazingly, it's a cheap Californian that I found at the marketplace. I just can't seem to adapt to retsina."

Lady Phillipa smiled. "Neither can I, and I've lived here at least half my life."

Sigourney crossed to the sagging wingback chair and offered one of the chipped glasses to her visitor. Not since her childhood had Sigourney lived under such Spartan conditions and once exposed to the best America and the rest of the world had to offer, she had sworn she would never let herself return to that earlier, brutal life. In recent years, her idea of roughing it was turning the electric blanket down to three.

Yet there she was, living on the very brink of death. And never had she felt so alive.

She slipped off her shoes and curled up in the dilapidated chair opposite Lady Phillipa. "I suppose it's common knowledge within your organization that Damon has persuaded me to cover the revolution?"

"We're very grateful, Sigourney—may I call you Sigourney?—for everything you're doing. I've managed to procure some identification papers for you and Damon." She smiled wryly. "The best forger in this part of Europe made them."

"When I leave Macedonia, I suppose I'll need them," Sigourney said, feeling that her smile was a bit too bright.

"Also, I've brought some clothing for both of you, since I doubt it would be wise to try to claim your luggage at airport customs."

"Well, I would like to retrieve my equipment bag. I feel lost without it."

Lady Phillipa's brow furrowed. "I know a man who used to be a children's photographer. Perhaps we can requisition a camera from him." She smiled then, adding, "And Damon can get you a tape recorder—unfortunately it won't record that much and the quality of the sound is usually poor, but it's designed to fit inside a cigarette package."

One more reminder of the world Damon inhabited: one where spying devices were commonplace. She recalled an innocuous-looking gadget Major Veronos had shown her at the training camp—the ultimate in spy gear—a plastic olive that concealed a sending device whose cocktail swizzle stick served as an antenna to transmit party conversations up to one hundred feet.

"You love him, don't you?" Sigourney asked with a trace of her old bluntness. "You love Damon."

Carefully, as if it were fine crystal, Lady Phillipa set aside her glass. "Oh, yes," she replied quietly, serenely. "But then, don't all women? Damon is the quintessential Mediterranean male and more. His subtler macho manner doesn't bowl a woman over like the more aggressive men do. Instead, it seduces us. His erotic voice communicates with women. When he smiles..."

Sigourney grinned. "It's so dazzlingly that, for safety's sake, it almost has to be viewed through smoked glass, like a solar eclipse."

Both women laughed, and then Lady Phillipa grew solemn. "But Damon has put himself on some plateau where emotion, as well as memory, is dead. I can't reach him, and I don't know if anyone else can. It's bloody difficult to compete with a memory, isn't it?" She ran a distracted hand through her short, stylishly cut hair. "God, I don't know why I am telling you this, a virtual stranger."

"I'm honored that you have. We can share our happiness with anybody. It's sharing the sadness and pain that matters."

Lady Phillipa picked up her glass. "Here's to Macedonia's liberation—and to our friendship, Sigourney Hamilton."

Sigourney's fingertip lightly traced the purple weal that meandered beneath one rib, close to his kidneys. Damon knew that she wanted to ask him how he had received that particular scar. His body was a collage of such grisly souvenirs. Instead, she reached for his shirt draped across the chair and passed it to him. She always managed to surprise him, never doing what he expected.

"Do not put on your clothes just yet," he told her, his voice languid.

"Again?" she teased. But her lovely smile, the result of their lovemaking, faded under his unsmiling gaze. Her lips wore the passion-bruised look of a woman whose desire has recently been gratified. The long sleep had made her look remarkably beautiful, even more so, if it were possible, than she was already.

She paused in drawing on her silky briefs and looked up at him from behind the sleek falling wave of her luxuriant hair, her tantalizingly tilted eyes questioning. Do you care for me at all? Can you ever love me? He knew what she was asking, and felt a moment of exasperation, mainly with himself.

"Why do I get the impression that the sight of my lush, naked body has nothing to do with your request?" she asked lightly.

"This man we are meeting today—I know little about this Albanian, except that five times now he has sold military information to the PFF, mostly closely guarded secrets dealing with the location of armories and arsenals, dates of gun shipments into the country, things of that nature. Most of the time the information panned out. But twice, when we sent a man to check the information, it seemed the VASIK were expecting the visit. Veronos suspects the Albanian of playing both sides. Today, I will force the man's hand."

She canted her head, eyes bright—with speculation or from their lovemaking, he couldn't tell. "There's something else, isn't there, Damon?"

"Yes."

He shrugged into the pin-striped oxford shirt without bothering to button it and crossed to the nightstand. "I am anticipating trouble, Sigourney. The place we are to meet, the National Gardens, may involve passing through at least one checkpoint. I might be searched, but I don't think you will be."

From the nightstand drawer he withdrew a tiny thin notebook like those used to record telephone numbers. "This is a code book that will be passed to our contact if I feel he's a safe risk."

She reached for her purse, and he said, "No. If you are searched, that would be the first place the guard would look." He knelt before her where she sat on the bed and picked up the lacy bra from the floor. "Put it on, but don't fasten it."

He watched as she complied with his request, her lovely eyes never once leaving his. When it was in place, he tucked the book between the bra's left cup and her breast. He felt the quickening of her breath at his touch on her flesh, and he intentionally latched the bra's front hooks with a brusque motion.

He rose and looked down at her, his eyes raking her lithe beauty. There was a part of him made soft by her, a part that he had closed off to love. If he were a man without a country, if there were a place without a past, he would answer her unspoken question. Yes, he could love her then. "I should make you go back to the United States."

The pale blue of her irises darkened, drawing him into the depths of her soul. "I'll go of my own accord, when I am ready to," she said simply, quietly.

He took her hands and pulled her roughly to her feet. She looked up at him with eyes that mirrored her trust in him. His palms pressed her temples, and he could detect the rapid thudding of her pulse. The feelings for her that he refused to identify warred with his need to use her for Macedonia's liberation. He told her as much, brutally, honestly.

"I am taking advantage of you, Sigourney. I am capitalizing on your love. It's unfair of me to make love to you. Do you understand? Something could happen to you. I do not want that. But it is going to be up to you to tell me no. Tell me!"

She cast him a beguilingly odd smile. Beneath the heavy fringe of sooty lashes, her light blue eyes contained an indefinable look. Sadness? Pity? Her hands slid about his neck, and she stood on tiptoe to press her mouth softly against the angry slash of his. His lips went pliant under the persistence of her kiss. How could he let her go? Yet to feel love now was almost traitorous...or was unfaithful a better word?

"Then use me," she whispered against the corner of his lips and stepped back, waiting.

He grabbed her arms, pulling her to him, and ravished her mouth. When the little moan of pleasure slipped from between her lips, he eased her back onto the bed. He was so hungry for her. Always. Despite the sense that his life was hovering on the edge of extinction, he was able to feel the intense joy of making love to this incredible woman.

Without a thought for the codebook, he lifted her breasts out of her bra and buried his head between them, until his mouth blindly sought a thickening, dusky rose nipple. His jaws flexed, tugging it as if to suck dry the love for him that filled her being.

His hand followed the line of her hip bone to cup her warmth through her delicate panties. She arched herself into his palm, welcoming the pressure of his blunt finger, which began a gentle rotating massage until he was rewarded with the moist evidence of her need for him. She smelled of his scent. The knowledge made him wild with wanting her.

The code book plopping to the floor brought him quickly back to his senses. He raised his head. Her eyes were glazed with desire, her lids heavy with languor.

"We will sit on a picnic bench before a small fountain, Sigourney," he told her crisply, drawing her back from some distant pastel world. With concentrated effort, her eyes focused on him.

"Albanion will sit opposite us," he continued, when he knew she was fully attentive. "You are to lean against me. I will rest my hand on your thigh. If at anytime I squeeze, you must duck beneath the picnic table. At once. Now put the dress on."

The code book's leather cover was hot and sweaty against her breast. She steeled herself to smile, to listen to Damon's descriptions of the sights of Constantine. They were just two tourists enjoying a sight-seeing holiday in the Macedonian capital. In her shoulder bag were the false papers procured for her by Lady Phillipa.

The dress she wore was a lovely raw silk creation of teal blue. The size was perfect. With certainty, she knew Lady

Phillipa had chosen the color with her in mind, most likely had purchased it from some haute couture establishment. The blue caught the elusive shade of her eyes and highlighted her unusual skin coloring, set off by the raven hair swaying against her shoulders as she walked beside Damon. With the dress's side slit and mandarin collar, her exotic beauty was displayed to its best advantage.

"During the Middle Ages," Damon was saying easily, a little louder than his normal speech, "the Fourth Crusade sacked Constantine in its battle against the sagging Byzantine Empire. The Crusaders carried back not only treasures and artifacts, but Aegean ideas that influenced the Western world—philosophy, government, drama and science."

As he had predicted, a checkpoint blocked the sidewalk at the intersection ahead. "Just keep walking," he said. "To turn around may draw unwanted attention."

Three armed soldiers guarded either side of the sawhorse barricade, while a fourth flipped through ID papers. An older man ahead of them was searched, apparently a random selection. She felt perspiration begin to gather between her breasts and dampen the insides of her thighs. Her circulation felt constricted. The little book secreted inside her bra seemed to burn her flesh.

Behind her, Damon's fingers on her upper arm tensed in readiness.

When her turn came, she presented her papers, smiled perfunctorily at the soldier and looked back at Damon with a mischievous wink. "When they search me, darling, you mustn't act jealous."

The baby-faced soldier chortled. "I would not dare make a man as big as he is jealous!"

The check was over in seconds. With the barricade behind her, she took a deep, gulping breath, afraid she was going to be sick.

"You should have been an actress instead of a journalist," Damon told her, circling a steadying arm about her waist.

They dodged the blue-and-white trolley buses darting down the main boulevard and crossed over to the marble-arched entrance to the National Park. There, a sponge seller lifted his featherweight bundles for customer inspection, and a bootblack capped his bottle with the brass end of a lightbulb. A vendor of roasted nuts jingled the drachmas in her apron pockets and a horde of pigeons flocked about her.

Within the grounds of the National Gardens, peacefulness was pervasive. A forest of huge, old trees cooled the shaded maze of winding brick walkways and blocked out the cacophony of the throbbing metropolis outside the grounds. Flowers of every type and color scented the air. The National Gardens covered more than three square miles, and one could stroll along the footpaths for half an hour without meeting another soul.

"Damon," she whispered. "your knife. You didn't bring it. What if there's trouble?..."

He glared down at her, eyes hard. "If there's trouble, we have to make do. Do you really think that access to protection—to a gun—is as easy here as it is in your country?''

''I'm tired of always having my American citizenship thrown up at me,'' she snapped.

''There is Greek blood in you, also,'' he drawled.

''And Korean and American,'' she bit back, her voice low so passersby wouldn't notice. Her anger was a good defense against her growing fear. She was so weary of being afraid, of marshaling resentment as a catalyst for her almost nonexistent courage.

As if sensing this, he touched her cheek and said gently, ''You are so pale, Sigourney. Do you want to wait for me at a nearby taverna?''

Her eyes jerked upward into his. ''No. You need me. What if this Albanian—'' She couldn't bring herself to voice her fear that Damon might be hurt. It would be unbearable to sit alone in some taverna, waiting for him—when he didn't show up. Ever. ''I'm coming with you.''

She would force herself to act bravely. She would have to anticipate Damon's anger, his desires, his actions. This would be an entirely new experience for her. She had always prided herself on her desirability and her skill at making the right choices in her life. She had been her own person. But Damon took her to places inside herself of which she had been totally unaware. Now she lived only to love him more each day.

Damon checked his watch. ''We're early. How does cotton candy sound?''

"Yummy." Her stomach was too nervous for anything heavier.

Through some inner divination, he led her to a small amusement park within the grounds. A little boy was tugging at his father's arm, and two gossiping mothers pushed infants in baby strollers. At a stand surrounded by clamoring children Damon purchased a cone of the pink, aromatic fluff. "To fatten you up," he teased, his smile dazzling.

She knew he was trying to relax her, but the code book between her breasts was a constant reminder of the covert life she had begun to lead.

"Why?" she asked, returning a forced smile. "Do you Macedonians really prefer tubby ladies?"

"Most certainly." He nodded toward a mustached man who was playing an accordion and singing. "Listen to the song's words."

"'I long to kiss your plump arms,'" she translated after a moment, smiling.

Damon dropped a couple of drachmas in the sandpail dangling from the man's shoulder strap. When the singer bobbed his head with a grateful grin, she recognized him from the taverna where she had been formally introduced to Damon. "You are being watched," the man murmured from between lips still stretched in a grin.

"Thank you," Damon said. "I will remember." He looked down at her. "It's time."

The peaceful interlude was over.

The fountain Damon had chosen for the meeting was

located in a circular flagstone pavilion. Several picnic tables were scattered around a grassy area fanning out from the building. Damon's fingers tightened about her hand, and she followed the direction of his stare.

A flower stall had been set up near the fountain, and in the absence of customers, the burly vendor was desultorily flipping through a porno magazine. So much for solitude.

All the picnic tables were empty but one. Still grasping her hand in his large one, Damon strode resolutely over to that table. "Papageorge, isn't it?" he asked.

The Albanian nodded. He was a dapper dresser and could have passed for a banker or a doctor or a lawyer—sure, a banker accused of embezzlement, a doctor who performed illegal abortions, a lawyer who bought off the police. The man lacked any trace of respectability, but she couldn't quite select any one physical characteristic that was responsible for his sleazy appearance.

After they were seated across from him, the Albanian asked, "You have come prepared to negotiate for the information?"

She leaned cozily against Damon, as he had instructed, and he rested his hand amorously on her thigh. She marveled that he could be so convincingly calm. Did he feign passion just as well?

"The information you have—is it worth the price?" Damon countered.

"It always has been before." The Albanian made a brave sweep of his hand.

Damon ignored the man's theatrics. "I wouldn't count the loss of our men worth the price. You must think we are very stupid."

The Albanian's smile was close to a sneer. "Desperate would, I believe, be a better word."

Damon shrugged his powerful shoulders. "Maybe. But we are not so desperate that we would buy from an informer."

The Albanian's close-set eyes flared at the insult.

"We will let you know whether we will or will not continue to deal with scum like you," Damon continued. She realized that he was deliberately baiting the man.

Suddenly, before she could comprehend exactly what was happening, the Albanian sprang to his feet. What followed seemed to occur in slow motion: frame by frame by frame. She saw fiery hatred in the man's eyes and a knife in his hand swiping straight at her chest.

Surely the man wouldn't really hurt her. She had nothing to do with this. She didn't even believe in bloodshed. She was just reporting events. She must be safe from harm.

Then she felt Damon's right hand shove violently at her shoulders. At the same time, the heel of his left hand caught the Albanian's jaw.

She was knocked under the picnic table. A shudder of fear, not unlike a sexual tremor, rippled through her. From her viewpoint, she spotted the flower vendor, behind the Albanian, raise a small automatic from under his counter. Illogically, hysterically, she hoped he didn't sneeze, because the gun might go off.

"Get out of here!" Damon shouted at her.

The Albanian crumpled to the ground. A thin cord of crimson circled his throat like a necklace of gore. His eyes were already glazing. Horrified, she scrambled to her feet when she saw Damon hurl a flowerpot at the stocky flower vendor. At the same time, a flash of orange exploded from the other man's pistol. She was frozen from shock. The flowerpot slammed into the man, and his pistol flew from his outstretched hand.

"Sigourney!"

She turned dazed eyes on Damon, and he yelled, "Do what I tell you. Get the hell out of here!"

She staggered back from the violence animating his face. At the same time he dove for the Albanian's pistol lying next to the picnic table leg. The vendor dashed over and wrestled with Damon. The two tumbled and rolled across the flagstone pavement and into the grass. The pistol went off with a booming report.

Then Damon was up and running, shoving and pulling her with him along an isolated footpath. They slammed into a male jogger in running shorts, who swore at them and shook his fist in an obscene gesture, but by then she really wasn't paying attention.

Scarlet was splotching Damon's oxford-cloth shirt on the left side, just below his ribs.

Safely back at the little flat, Damon poured her a stiff brandy. She swallowed it down and said, "I'm all right, now. But you're not.'' She nodded at the strips of bed-sheet she had wrapped about his ribs. ''If there's a bullet in you, it needs to come out.''

He tossed down his own drink. ''Father Murphy's had emergency first-aid training. We will leave it until he arrives.''

He went over to the coffee table and picked up the pistol he had fought so hard to get. On rubbery legs she joined him and watched with a detachment born of shock as he field-stripped the weapon with a few quick, expert motions.

What had happened an hour earlier still seemed unreal. Only what went on in the apartment was real. Only what she felt for Damon was real.

''At least we have this gun,'' he said. ''It is one more than we did have. And there are two less men to betray us to the other side.''

He looked up and saw pallor in her face. ''Kiss me, Sigourney.''

That was exactly what she wanted, needed. To be held in the protective embrace of his mighty arms. Her lips lifted and sought the narcotic kiss that would wipe out all that had occurred that afternoon.

His lips slid gently over hers, whispering her name against her mouth while he cradled her. She could feel his passion taking hold of him, and she thrilled at the knowledge that—always—he wanted her.

Her lower body arched wantingly into his. Coursing through her was the desperate need to be one with him.

This time she didn't want any preliminaries. She wanted him just to take her.

"Please, Damon…" she begged in a low, raspy voice she wouldn't have recognized as belonging to her. "Please, love me quickly. Now."

He raised his head and just for a moment she caught in his eyes the tenderness of which she knew he was capable. "You are too vulnerable, Sigourney. Now, now that you have been through a gun-battle with me, you should be leaving, going back to the United States as fast as you can. Instead, I am keeping you here, taking advantage of the trauma you have just undergone because I want you so badly."

"I always feel off-balance with you," she whispered. She shook her head, as though she could shake off the bemusement that held her enthralled. "With you I find myself at the mercy of some instinct I don't quite understand."

"I understand it, though." He smiled, smoothing back her hair and tucking it behind her ear. "What you feel after being confronted by death is the same thing that soldiers feel. After a gesture of destruction, they must perform the gesture of creation. It is the basic biological—"

A knock at the door cut him off. "It's your neighborhood priest," the gruff voice said from the hallway. "Collecting tithes for the needy."

Damon released her reluctantly and opened the door for Father Murphy, who was carrying an oversized family bible. The priest took one look at her and said, "You look like you could use a drink, my child. I certainly could."

She smiled weakly. "I think you're right. Brandy okay with you?"

"Brandy? My oh my, it's been ages since I've tasted such sacred firewater."

"Damon? Do you want a refill?"

He shook his head, and a clump of butter-churned curls fell across his wide forehead. "Later."

"See to Damon, will you, Father, while I pour. He won't hold still under my ministrations."

When she handed him his glass, the priest had just unwrapped the linen bandages. "Who shot you?"

"I did not see."

"Well, it stands to reason, doesn't it? After all, you have earned a reputation for that sort of social excess."

"Please." Damon grimaced when the priest yanked off the remaining strip with a little less than a doctor's bedside finesse. "No sermons."

She wasn't surprised when Father Murphy opened the bible and removed from its hollowed interior a pair of surgical scissors, along with an impressive array of medical paraphernalia.

Unable to bring herself to watch him administer first aid, she went to the window and looked out, while quickly finishing off her second glass of brandy. She felt steadier and more in control. But when Damon groaned, she flinched. She stifled a protest at the crude surgery Father Murphy was forced to perform and instead lit two cigarettes, one for Damon and the other for herself.

When it was all over and Father Murphy took his leave several hours later, she closed the door and turned back to Damon. He lay in the bed. Beneath his tan, his flesh had turned gray. His ribs, resembling a whiskey barrel, had been rebandaged. His magnificent body would mend rapidly, but the tightness at the corners of his mouth told her that he was suffering at the moment.

She went to the nightstand and picked up the battered bullet the priest had pried out of his wound. For a long moment she studied it. She knew that Damon was studying her, too. He must have a fairly good notion of what she was thinking.

With restless anticipation, she put the bullet down and looked at him. "If I left now, Damon," she said in what she hoped was a calm voice, "you wouldn't try to stop me, would you?"

His irises went cold and almost black. Empty. "No."

Her brain felt as if it were being pleated like an accordion bellows. "Some day, Damon, you're going to need someone, and I hope to God that someone will be there to respond."

"Sigourney, you are wanting from me what I cannot give."

"Then I pity you."

His voice was matter-of-fact. "When you leave, get Phillipa to go with you to the airport. She has a contact there who can slip you through customs."

"Oh, I'm not leaving, Damon. At least, not yet. I'm going to stay with you until the moment comes when I know you face certain death. It might be tomorrow, it might be six months from now. But when that time comes, then I'll leave. I love you, but not enough to watch you die." She gave him a sad half-smile. "Or maybe too much."

Chapter 10

Damon seemed never to tire, or to need sleep. He was addicted to his own adrenaline. He stood, looking out of the apartment's darkened window sluiced by September's dismal drizzle, and Sigourney wondered what webs of plots and tricks his intricate mind was spinning. She noticed that he chain-smoked now. And she noticed again that his physique was phenomenal. Naked, he prowled the apartment like a mighty mastiff. His body resembled a Da Vinci anatomical drawing of a perfect man, striated with ropes of muscles.

She saw that his golden curls had crept past his nape and needed shearing. She denied herself the urge to go to him and instead stayed in bed, her back bolstered by both pillows. Father Murphy's warning, "Damon cannot stand for people to try to get too close to him," was always with her.

How long could she survive on hope alone, hope that one day this self-sufficient man would need her? Oh, she knew that he wanted her, that he cared for her. His demonstrations of deep tenderness led her to suspect that he might even love her. But she wanted him to need her—not for what she could do for his precious cause, but for what she could be to him and for him.

She was merely incidental to his life and mission, which were one and the same.

She bent her head so that the cascade of hair concealed the intense longing etched on her face and went back to her writing.

Forty-five minutes later, she knew he had resolved whatever problem had been teasing him. He crossed to the bed and, one knee braced on the mattress, knelt over her. "Your columns have been stirring interest all over the world, Sigourney."

"Oh?" Macedonia censored the radio and television and newspapers, so she was often unaware of what was going on in the rest of the world. But Damon seemed to have a direct line in and out.

"I have been contacted by agents of Sheikh Ibrahim Rajhi. He has expressed an interest in investing his petrodollars in our little revolution."

She remembered the Arab merchant from a series she had done on King Saud. Sheikh Rajhi had made a fortune in arms dealing. At one time all Saudi arms purchases had been channeled through him, as well as the purchase of planes and military vehicles. The affluent Arab speculator had also made loans to America's automotive and computer industry giants, and was the largest private shareholder, after a former United States vice-president, in a major Manhattan bank.

"Why?"

"He is banking that the eventual payoff will be lucrative. Or at least I hope to convince him of that. I am going to pay him a visit."

"I'm going with you."

His admiring gaze swept over the milk white globes partially covered by the muslin sheet, and he stiffened with excitement. "Not right now, Sigourney; for now we are not going anywhere but to bed."

Sheikh Rajhi arranged for one of his fleet of executive jets, a Gulfstream G-III, to pick them up at a small airstrip on Rhodes. The trip via trawler from an isolated cove on Macedonia's southern coast to the political asylum of Rhodes had been a dangerous crossing made at night. A Macedonian cutter had spotted the trawler when the cloud-covering momentarily lifted. From there it had been a deadly serious game of dodge and hide-and-seek as the cloud-covering came and went.

Even now, as the Gulfstream's seat belt light went off, she didn't feel completely safe, but she said nothing of her lingering terror to Damon. No other passengers were aboard, just the crew of two and the cabin attendant—a young, attractive Swiss girl who served them from a full galley. There were stereo and video systems in addition to a full-sized bathroom.

During the flight, the darkness below was lit intermittently by gas flares from the Saudi Arabian oil fields. As the Gulfstream swept in over Dubai, the Arab emirate on the Persian Gulf might have been Los Angeles. The lights of its bungalows and highways stretched an extraordinary distance into the soft night of the desert.

Sigourney buckled her seat belt for the landing. The digital clock on the front bulkhead displayed half past nine, and beside her Damon dozed, something he hadn't done the night before. While she was sleeping, he had gone over a French pamphlet on the international currency market in preparation for the meeting with the Arab businessman.

The Gulfstream touched ground with scarcely a bump, and Damon's lids snapped open. Without glancing at him, she knew he was instantly awake and rested.

The jet rolled to a halt on a side runway that was awash with private jets, the tails of which were emblazoned with their owners' initials. When the hatch swung open, the cabin attendant bade Sigourney and Damon good-bye. Sigourney didn't miss the lusty stare the buxom silver-blonde turned on Damon. His undisguised sexuality appealed to females of all ages. To the hostess's regret, Damon barely acknowledged her toothpaste smile.

At the private hangar a heavily armored deep red Mercedes 300 awaited them. The humid Persian Gulf heat made breathing an agony for Sigourney, and she was grateful for the luxurious limousine's blasting air conditioning.

Rows of towering royal fan palms marked the main boulevard from the airport into the city. The car circumvented the *souqs* and nightclubs of downtown Dubai and made its way toward the armpit of the Persian Gulf, which had once been infamous as the Pirate Coast.

What struck Sigourney most about Dubai was not its regal splendor but its disorder—uncompleted roads, open garbage dumps, painfully smashed-up and abandoned cars, the unfleshed skeletons of concrete buildings. Everything looked half-finished. Closer to the harbor rose the squat office buildings and plants of American oil companies.

At a pier made of basalt rock, a sharklike black power boat shared the dark waters with a school of wooden, sharp-prowed sailing dhows. Damon helped her board the sleek speedboat. Quickly it began to cruise out into the sultry darkness, piloted by a silent Arab garbed in Western clothing and wearing the traditional headdress of red and white cloth tucked into black-ribbed headropes, exposing his leathered neck.

Standing next to Damon, she felt the blessing of the breeze whipping the dampness from her hair. Soon brilliant lights in the distance signaled their approach to the sheikh's yacht. Despite the late hour, three watchful men in dark glasses with cropped hair and suntans ushered them aboard.

Sigourney drew a deep breath of admiration. What she saw could have been a scene from a James Bond movie.

The *Houri* was several hundred feet of polished gray steel with bronze reflective windows. At the bow of the vessel was a white communications pod linking the sheikh's telephone and telex lines by satellite to his other boats, planes, cars and bases around the world.

At her side, Damon said a little bitterly, "I estimate there is at least twenty-five million dollars tied up in this little toy. Think of what Macedonia could do with that for defense."

In the pile-carpeted staterooms, *Star Wars* seemed a better comparison than *Dr. No.* Doors slid open by remote control, and some of them functioned only when one of the three bodyguards tapped out the right code on calculator buttons set where the handles usually were.

A smiling Sheikh Ibrahim Rajhi greeted them in a room devoted to video game machines. Portly, with an undisciplined, wispy beard and thick round glasses, he looked owlish. He certainly was not the stuff about which pulp novels were written. Urbane, intelligent, Westernized, he looked incongruous at the control panel of "Space Invaders."

"*Salaam,*" Sheikh Rajhi said.

"And upon you be peace," replied Damon mechanically. He dwarfed the sheikh.

Once the amenities were over, the sheikh said with an expansive sweep of his hand, "You must see the rest of my yacht, then a repast and bed. Tomorrow we will deal with business concerns, my friends."

The sheikh was a bluff, gregarious guide, overflowing with energy. The yacht's command room was similar to that of the Star Ship *Enterprise*. In the teakwood command room telex and wire services, including API and UP, clattered away, unattended. The sheikh's personal masseur came with the gymnasium, as did the barber and a rather old-fashioned barber's chair. A tiny movie theater was darkened, but in a marbled discotheque illuminated panels reflected the frenetic movements of couples gyrating to hard rock music.

"What are you celebrating?" Sigourney asked.

The sheikh shrugged and lifted his palms. "A wedding, a death, the unveiling of a statue—whatever excuse one ever finds for a party."

On the fifth and top deck, beside the swimming pool, was the sheikh's helicopter pad. "My nephew is presently using the helicopter, but he will return tomorrow," their host explained.

The "repast" he had planned was, simply put, sumptuous. They were entertained in the *majlis*, or reception room, where, following the sheikh and Damon's example, Sigourney kicked off her shoes and seated herself cross-legged before a low, black enameled table. A mound of cumin-flavored white rice moated with butter was set on one part of the table. Rising on another was a pyramid of steaming sheep ribs.

The sheikh and Damon rolled back their sleeves and picked up the hard pink crescents and began to eat. Noting with some unease the centerpiece of boiled sheep head, its tongue curling between glistening white teeth and bared gums, Sigourney reluctantly joined them.

Her appetite flagged sooner than that of the two men. When they, too, sat back replete, a servant brought lemon-scented fingerbowls. The meal was followed by cups of tea, a few jokes, and some stories, all of which Damon handled like a skilled diplomat.

For her own part, Sigourney interjected only a few observations. In the Arab estimation, a silent woman was worth rubies. Normally Sigourney would have matched the sheikh barb for barb, but she didn't want to jeopardize Damon's business venture.

A boy appeared bearing a small silver brazier holding smoking incense, and that was the signal to retire. Their stateroom was opulent, as she had expected. Royal purple draperies swathed the walls and matched the lush carpet. A mauve spread covered a round bed of stupendous dimensions. Alone with Damon, she risked a glance at the mirrored ceiling. In its reflection his satyr's gaze met hers. He grinned. "I think the yacht is appropriately named."

His eyes sobered, and he turned to her with an outward grace and inward power that were ineluctible. Unwillingly, she trembled in excited anticipation. He took her palms in his hands and kissed first one, then the other, his hot-eyed gaze pinning her where she stood. She was aware of a drumming in her ears that could only be the blood thundering through her arteries.

Slowly his fingers began to undo her blouse buttons; they gave one by one, like falling dominoes. "What a man enjoys most about a woman's clothes, Sigourney, are his fantasies of how she will look without them. You are far lovelier than any of my fantasies.''

His low, resonant voice set off a vibration deep within her stomach, and she moaned softly when he brushed aside her heavy hair to bare her neck for his fiery kiss. A woman in love, she opened herself to him.

Afterward, she lay looking up at the two images in the mirrors, the naked bodies sprawled in a passionate pas de deux. She felt his essence settling inside her. She would hold it there, keeping it, even when she could not have him incarnate.

Reflected above her, a naked, bronzed Damon, asleep on his stomach, entrapped her with one arm flung across her ribs. It might as well have been a steel bar. Her love for this outlaw was building a cage around her. That night, as on other nights, she tried to deal with feelings she had never known before.

Her mind spun with unanswered questions. Did she have free will any longer? Could she fight against what seemed fated? Would she ever get enough of him? Could she escape this madness?

His soft, steady breathing was warm on her temple. She had forgotten the sensation of being held by a man, forgotten the muscular feel of a male chest and thighs. With him she did what she had never done before in the arms of a man. She lost her sense of balance, her sense of time and place. Sleeping in his arms, she felt a security and safety she had never known as a child.

And if he uttered "my love" in the midst of their lovemaking—well, she could take his meaning any way she wished.

She need only turn her face slightly upward to find his lips and the reassurance of his kiss. But she didn't want to awaken him, because she wanted to savor this hour wrapped in his arms. Soon enough he would open his eyes and leave her.

Still, her fingers, with what seemed a will of their own, tentatively grazed the hard, muscled ridge of his shoulders, and he stirred, his hand clamping about her wrist and bringing her palm to his lips, where he laved it with his tongue.

"Damon," she breathed. "Love me."

Intense white heat and bright color. Turquoise sea, cobalt sky, saffron sun. The merciless equatorial sun beat down on the yacht's deck, and the dozen or so anonymous guests cavorted in the Olympic-sized pool to escape the broiling rays. Their shouts and laughter were absorbed by the torpid afternoon air.

One of the two speedboats, having been lowered into the water by winches, darted about the yacht, towing intrepid water skiers. Sigourney felt there was something almost tawdry about this soft living. Especially now that her life consisted of only the barest essentials.

Beneath the shade of a large table parasol, she and Damon drank iced tea with Sheikh Rajhi, who today wore the traditional *dishdasha*, a full-length, shirtlike garment, and an outer robe or cloak known as a *mishlah*.

She wore one of several swimsuits she'd found in the stateroom, a sleek, white maillot, which, despite the laced slits down either side, more discreetly covered her anatomy than did the daring string bikinis worn by the other female guests. Keeping her face in the shade, she stretched out her legs to absorb some sunshine. Her ebony hair, lifted off her shoulders, was draped over the back of the deck chair.

Beside her, Damon idly lit one of his strong Turkish cigarettes, though she doubted that complex mind of his was as idle as his body appeared. The matchbook he had used was engraved with the sheikh's initials, the same stylized engraving found on the tail of his jet.

The swim trunks Damon wore, smoke blue Italian briefs, rode tantalizingly low on his hips, and she ached to run her fingertips over his velvet flesh, a toasted shade except for the various colored scars ranging from white to pink to purple, which she recognized as the most recent.

In his role as host, Sheikh Rajhi was graciously explaining the sight off the yacht's starboard side. A large dhow, with fifteen to twenty oars swinging in unison on each side, glided by not three hundred yards from the yacht.

"We are anchored over the Persian Gulf pearl banks, the richest in the world," he said.

She noticed that he directed his attention mostly to her, and her woman's instincts suspected that he had taken a special liking to her.

"If you watch," the sheikh pointed out, "the oars will be fixed horizontally with heavy stones on ropes tied to them."

The spectacle was truly fascinating, but she sensed that the shrewd old Arab was tactically delaying negotiations; however, she listened politely.

"The men you see in swim trunks," the sheikh said, "they will put wooden stoppers in their noses—look, see what they're doing now."

Intrigued, she watched as the divers took advantage of the stone weights to sink below the sea's blue-green surface.

"They go down forty feet or more," the sheikh continued, "and for two minutes, perhaps longer, they cut and pull oysters into a basket until their breath gives out."

Her attention, along with that of Damon and Sheikh Rajhi, was diverted from the exhibition by a whirring noise coming from the sky. She turned toward the sound and spotted a helicopter approaching.

"My nephew," the sheikh told them, and instantly she knew that the nephew's absence had been the reason for the delay in negotiations.

A black-haired, mustached man alighted and ducked to avoid the spinning blades as he made his way across the pad. Behind him sauntered a young Amazon of a woman, holding her platinum hair, styled in a page-boy, to keep it from blowing. The backlash of the rotors whipped her frothy scarlet dress above her knees, revealing gorgeous legs.

Sigourney's attention returned to the handsome man. Lean and rangy, he wore a three-piece gray suit, the hand-stitched mohair combat dress of the Western business-man. With the swashbuckling walk of the typical arro-gant Arab, he strolled toward them.

The sheikh rose to embrace his nephew. They hugged each other gently, and the sheikh kissed him on the fore-head and rubbed noses with him, eyes open.

Now that the nephew was closer, she could tell that he was much younger than she, perhaps in his mid- or late-twenties. His dark brown eyes were enormous.

"My nephew, Khalid Rajhi," the old Arab said.

Khalid met Damon's eyes with an insolent stare. Sig-ourney watched Damon acknowledge the introduction with the merest nod of his head. His face, as always, was closed, and his eyes, now a hard blue, inventoried the other man with that assessment that could be so harrow-ing to the person under scrutiny. So, Damon also knew that results depended on this brash young Arab.

For herself, Khalid's nostrils flared in tribute to her sex. His smile was engaging. She knew that smile well and interpreted it to mean, "You are but a mere woman, though a very beautiful one." Khalid's kind was always happy to pleasure a woman, but only because it reaf-firmed their own sexuality.

He turned to the woman standing behind him, who tried vainly to smooth her wind-tousled hair. Her baby face featured pouting, pink-glossed lips. "Go for a swim, Babette," he ordered in French.

"But I don't know how to swim, Khalid," she said in a kewpie-doll voice.

"Then get a suntan," he snapped impatiently, pulling out a chair for himself and leaving her standing.

After a second of bewilderment, she whirled with an "Ohh!" and stalked away.

"Get rid of that one," his uncle said. "She has no class."

After a boy in sandals and white cotton trousers brought Khalid a glass of iced tea, its sides already streaming with condensed moisture, the sheikh asked Damon in English, "Shall we do business now? My nephew is a graduate of one American university and one British one—Oxford—and I value his opinion. For this reason, I have summoned him. I believe your country—your underground movement—is in need of some financial backing?"

"We need arms for defense," Damon said flatly. "Nine-millimeter Uzi semiautomatic rifles, G-3 machine guns and M2s. And ammunition. Whatever you can arrange for us to smuggle into Macedonia."

Khalid leaned forward. "Tell me why my uncle should help you?"

"Because he has one hundred million dollars whose value he must maintain against inflation, and there are not that many safe and profitable investments around. Brazil, Mexico, Taiwan—he doesn't have a sporting chance of getting his money back, much less the interest, there. I believe your economics professor would call it recycling,'' Damon finished with an edge of sarcasm to his voice.

Now she understood why he had spent half the night studying the article on monetary issues and the international currency market.

Sheikh Rajhi fingered his worry beads as he talked, speaking slowly, with the deliberation of someone who has grown used to his slightest word being seized on and turned into banner headlines.

''It would be a substantial loan. In the short term, I am making a sacrifice. I could easily find more profitable outlets for a million or so dollars. But in the long term— I think it would be little sacrifice.''

''We do what we can for third-world nations,'' Khalid said, his smile taunting.

Damon turned an implacable gaze on the young Arab. ''We do not like being patronized.''

Khalid summoned his best desert-killer glare, but his uncle said unctuously, ''There are, of course, certain terms which must be met.''

Damon raised a brow. ''Which are?''

''My nephew will make the arms purchase and accompany the shipment to its distribution point in your country. In addition, if Miss Hamilton will consent, I would like for her to remain with my nephew through this process.''

Sigourney started at the unexpected reference to herself. Damon's expression didn't alter. ''She is not necessary as a hostage to ensure that your nephew will not be double-crossed. There are others with the PFF who would volunteer to accompany him.''

''You love Miss Hamilton?''

''My personal life is not open to discussion.''

''She is your woman?''

Sigourney felt as if she didn't exist for the three men. Khalid's handsome face was rigid with offended pride that he should be appointed as companion to a woman; Damon's expression was one of contained anger; behind his thick lenses, the sheikh's enlarged eyes blinked solemnly.

A tight knot coiled at the pit of her stomach as she waited an eternity for her lover's answer. The sunlight, now sneaking below the umbrella's canvas valance, was unbearably hot. The lower half of her right temple throbbed with a growing migraine, and with sure knowledge she knew she didn't want to hear Damon's answer.

''I am my own woman,'' she interrupted in a calm, controlled voice.

The sheikh nodded in the sage manner of an ancient caliph. ''I thought as much. I know you by reputation. A very sensible woman.''

He returned his attention to Damon. ''A very sensible woman when not in love. You are dangerous for her. When this revolution of yours begins—''

''It is not my revolution. When it does begin, I want the weapons for defense only.''

''Insh'allah,'' the sheikh replied, with a noncommittal lift of his narrow shoulders.

It was the Muslim's answer to almost every question about the future. "As God wills."

The sheikh tapped a knuckle on the rim of his tea glass for emphasis. "As you pointed out, there is a need for self-defense. My nephew will see to it that Miss Hamilton remains alive. And her presence will protect Khalid."

"And protect your investment in the weapons," Damon pointed out.

"The two are intertwined."

Damon's shuttered dark eyes swung toward her. Damn it, she thought, what was going on behind his iron facade?

"He is right," Damon said. "I am dangerous for you. It would be best if you forget even this business proposal. It would be best if you returned to the United States."

"But I won't."

He was angry. She could see past the dark blue of the irises; the black depths of his eyes might have been smoldering with the fumes of hell itself. He could make her leave, but he wouldn't, and for this he was angry with himself.

He shrugged his massive shoulders and with irony said, *"Insh'allah."*

Chapter 11

Sigourney was doing this for Damon. He had not asked her, would not, but he needed her to fulfill the conditions of Sheikh Rajhi's agreement by accompanying his nephew on the arms purchase trip. That was enough for her.

So she sat there with the handsome Arab playboy in Burgos, an Iberian city of tumbling red tile roofs and crumbling sandstone steps. This ancient village in northern Spain had held the royal quarters of King Ferdinand and Queen Isabella, and its inhabitants had welcomed Columbus on his return from his second trip to the New World. They had fought alongside El Cid, and warred against the Moorish invaders.

This was wine country on the edge of the Basque region, a territory of somber people and deep-running emotions.

From the leaded casement window of the Almirante Bonifaz's bar she watched desultorily as laundry fluttered like brilliant banners from the terraced apartments across the street. Opposite her, Khalid drank his glass of ruby port, his mouth sullen beneath the sweep of his mustache.

He was such a boy in some ways. Cocky as a Hollywood discovery, he was subtly disdainful of her—and resentful that she showed no interest in him as a member of the supreme sex. By the time their flight had touched down at Madrid's Barajas Airport, he had barely been conversing with her. During the four-hour drive north from the Spanish capital in a rented Renault, he had informed her only that on the following day they were to deal with a representative for the Basque ETA, a militant group demanding separation from Spain.

Why Khalid was dealing with the Basques she didn't know, but she supposed it had something to do with the laundering of money.

"I thought Muslims didn't drink," she said, nodding toward his empty glass.

He fastened those gorgeous brown eyes on her and flashed a charming smile. So, he would try the age-old tactics again. "Muslims are not required to run Christianity's never-ending spiritual obstacle course. Do not assume that the faith is weak just because the flesh is. Besides, which is worse, a bit of secret drinking behind closed doors or widespread alcoholism?"

"Isn't that a little hypocritical?"

"A little hypocrisy is a small enough price to pay to keep out the evils that plague your country—mugging, drug addiction, gang warfare and everything else that goes with an unregulated society."

She laughed. "I should know better than to argue with a True Believer."

A waiter in a red vest appeared to refill their glasses, and she watched in rapidly mounting distress as the raffia container bobbled in his fingers. Before he regained a firm hold, droplets of red wine had splashed over the bodice of her ivory wool dress, part of the meager but elegant wardrobe provided by Lady Phillipa.

Khalid shot to his feet. His hand knotted in the front of the flustered waiter's vest. *"Wallahi!"* he cursed. "By God, you have offended the lady."

The startled waiter almost dropped the bottle a second time. Patrons, scattered among the other tables, swung shocked eyes toward the disruption.

"Please, Khalid," she hissed, "it was a mistake!" With her napkin, she dabbed mechanically at the spots. She was frantic to be gone from the place. "He meant no harm."

"There is such a thing as respect. Apologize, pig!"

The poor man was trembling. Beads of perspiration glistened at his receding hairline. *"Por favor, señorà,* I am sorry!"

"No se preocupe. Es nada," she reassured the flustered waiter and, rising, flung her napkin on the table and hurried away.

Khalid tossed down a pocketful of pesetas and stalked after her. At the curb, he caught up with her. She wouldn't look at him, but signaled anxiously for one of the darting black taxis.

He took her upper arm. "Look, I am sorry if I have upset you."

She averted her gaze. Angry splotches heated the skin over her cheekbones. "You humiliated that man! There was no need for that!"

He propelled her toward their blue Renault. "You don't know that."

She compressed her lips and let him usher her into the little car. When he slid behind the wheel, he said, "You are now on the Macedonian Intelligence's wanted list, Miss Hamilton. VASIK would hire an agent to take you as a hostage—or as a corpse. Anyone is suspect of being in their employ. Anyone! It is my job to protect you."

"I can take care of myself, thank you."

He drove toward the outskirts of Burgos, where many of the cottages sported the owners' coats of arms. "That wasn't the agreement my uncle made with—"

"With my lover," she supplied, wanting to prick Khalid's inflated masculine ego.

"What makes him so special a man?" he demanded, his eyes flashing.

Her anger evaporated. She closed her eyes and rested her head against the back of the seat. "He is selfless, Khalid. And brilliant and strong and totally unaware of his power over the female sex."

For the moment that silenced the young Arab.

Landa Palace, where they were to spend the night, was actually a restored castle, or at least a portion of it had been restored: one tower and its surrounding courtyard. Nestled among softly wrinkled hills, the castle reminded her of a Mexican villa, with the lush greenery that overflowed the native-tiled corridors and the bright reds and yellows and oranges that splashed the stucco walls.

Instead of dining with him in the hotel restaurant, as Khalid politely suggested, she retired to her room, which had old-fashioned hot waterpipes as part of its decor. She wasn't sleepy, but she wasn't up to coping further with Khalid, either. He had vacillated between insolence and adulation. She wanted only to be alone with her thoughts of Damon.

Where was he tonight? In Lindos, with Sophie and Sotoris? At the training camp with Melina? With his parents in their bucolic mountain village? With Lady Phillipa?

It was better not to let herself dwell on what she could do nothing about. Soon, perhaps within hours, she could be on her way back to him.

She switched off the lamp and slipped between the bed's crisp sheets. With her hands cupped behind her head, she willed herself to sleep. In the room adjoining hers she could hear Khalid moving around. Her thoughts drifted to Father Murphy. She missed his levity; his wry humor eased the utter hopelessness of her love for Damon.

If she had any sense left, she would catch the first flight out of Madrid for the States. But she had only love in her, and she would stay with Damon until she knew that his end was near.

End? she thought contemptuously, and fumbled on the nightstand for a cigarette and her lighter. What had happened to her reporter's cool objectivity? Why didn't she use the correct term?

Death.

She couldn't imagine Damon dead, his flesh cold. He was too vital, too alive. If he died, there would be no place in the world for her to run.

The thought of Damon dead was so horrifying that she slid out of the bed and began to pace the room. In the darkness, the cigarette in her hand glowed, melding with the faint moonlight filtering through the curtain sheers.

At the knock on the connecting door, she turned. After a long moment, she asked, "Yes?"

Khalid's voice was muffled. "Are you all right?"

"Yes. I just wasn't sleepy."

"Neither am I. I will talk with you until you grow tired."

Her brows knitted at the suggestion. Still, she was too restless to sleep. "All right," she said, and went to unlock the connecting door.

She wore only a brown satin teddy, but the room was relatively dark; besides, the teddy covered more of her than the sleek, white maillot Khalid had seen her in aboard the *Houri*. She smiled to herself at the Arabic word, which was frequently interpreted as meaning a luscious and shapely nymph but really meant the spiritual companion the good Muslim expected to meet in paradise.

She was willing to bet that it was not spiritual companionship Khalid expected from her.

For several seconds he stood looking at her, and she wondered uneasily if she had made a mistake in admitting him to her room. But, no, he would protect her with his life. She was certain of it. Not because he cared about her, but because he had been entrusted with that duty, and his Arab pride would not let him consider any alternative.

She padded over to the blue chintz loveseat and drew her legs under her. "You said you weren't sleepy. Are you concerned about the meeting tomorrow?" She tried to keep the anxiety from her voice. What if something went wrong and Damon didn't get the weapons he so badly needed for defense?

Khalid crossed to the matching tufted chair and settled his lean frame into it. "No more than usual. There is always an element of danger."

After he lit a cigarette and exhaled, he said, "I was born and spent my childhood in a goat-hair tent, knowing the smell of camel dung and the taste of sand and the feel of constant danger. The post oil-embargo boom changed the first two; the danger is always present."

She suspected that he was trying to impress her, but listening to him would take her mind off Damon. "Tell me more."

"I can tell you everything you ever wanted to know about camels." His soft laughter was deprecatory, and for once there was no trace of condescension in his voice. "Everyone knows that the camel can go without drinking for a long time—six weeks if the vegetation is good—but did you know it can convert that vegetation and undrinkable brackish water into top-quality milk? Or that when you're starving, even camel hooves can be ground into powder and baked into cakes? Or that their urine can be used to bathe your—"

"Please," she said.

He laughed again. Moonlight dusted his dark face, and she thought not for the first time that he would make a fantastic male model. He was beautiful, but completely masculine.

"Then shall I tell you instead about tracking footprints in the sand, Miss Hamilton? Even before desert children learn to ride, they are taught to track camel footprints. The children can determine if the beast was ridden or served as a pack animal. You see, riding camels are females, pack animals are bulls."

His voice dropped an octave. "And now that I have mentioned females, did you know that certain Bedouin tribes can track a woman and tell if she is a virgin or not? A maiden has a certain way of holding her legs when she walks that a woman who has known a man does not."

If he expected her to react with embarrassment, he would be disappointed. "You're simply full of wondrous information, Khalid."

"I'm no longer a dumb little camel boy, Miss Hamilton. I know a good deal about the world of high finance and high society. I have heard of you. You are a famous woman." There was grudging respect in his voice.

"Coming from you, a male chauvinist, that's quite a compliment."

"You are also very brave for a woman."

This time she laughed aloud. "Why do you say that? Because I entrust my virtue to a playboy like you?"

"No. Because what you are doing is risky. If you return to Macedonia, if General Agamemnon's agents—"

She held up her palms. "Please, I'm a dyed-in-the-wool coward. Let's not talk about danger, or I won't sleep a wink tonight."

He leaned forward and asked earnestly, "Why have you given up your work to follow him? You had everything you could want. I do not understand this."

"I love Damon Demetrios. That is the only answer."

"That is all?"

She laughed a little sadly. "No, I suppose I am somewhat mad. What I probably need is electro-shock therapy."

"This kind of love is beyond my comprehension."

She stabbed out her cigarette in a baked clay ashtray on the end table. "I understand where you're coming from, friend. I was there once myself. I wish I still were."

She rose and stretched, covering a yawn that was cut short by the burning look in the dark eyes that traveled over her bare thighs and satin-covered breasts. Another time, before Damon, she might have entertained the idea of a flirtation with this young man, though she doubted she would have carried that speculation to fruition.

She walked to the door and opened it. "I think I can sleep now, Khalid. Good night."

He stood, but did not follow her to the door. Hands on his hips, he tilted his head to one side, as though considering something. "You called me friend. All right, I will be one. Until I'm ready to be more." Only then did he leave the room.

Shutting and latching the door after him, she had to smile. Khalid ibn Rajhi was not only planning to protect her, he was planning to seduce her. For once her feminine vanity was gratified by a man's attentions. She certainly could do with a dose of flattery.

"You are very beautiful," Khalid complimented her the next day. She wore a Blass dress of mauve Ultrasuede with a burgundy chiffon sash.

"Thank you," she said crisply, "Shall we go?" She was a little nervous about what Khalid planned to do. Purchasing large quantities of arms was something on which most governments frowned.

Khalid drove through the Rioja vineyard district, a rugged area in the heart of Old Castile, halfway between Madrid and the French border. Once, after they crossed an arched, wooden bridge, he abruptly swung the car off the road behind a brake of willow bushes.

When he turned around in the seat to look behind them, she asked, "What is it?"

He merely held up a silencing hand.

Within a minute or so another car passed by, traveling fast. "Do you think we were being followed?" she persisted, an uneasy feeling worming up her spine.

His shoulders lifted in that gesture of fatalism common to the Middle East. "Anything is possible."

The magnificent house to which he took her resembled a French chateau, all dapper gray and pristine white and rose pink. Below the quaintly decorated tiled mansard roof, late autumn flowers filled numerous window boxes.

A middle-aged woman in a starched black dress admitted them to the foyer, where they were soon greeted by an elderly man in a black beret tilted rakishly above a roguish mustached face, not the sort she would have thought would be an arms dealer.

Khalid introduced him as Señor Curro Aulestia. The Basque opened his arms expansively and enfolded Khalid in the customary *abrazo* of the country. "Your uncle has told me you wished to tour our wine cellars. We produce and age our own wines here, you know. Come, let me show you and your friend around."

They followed their host across a marbled floor, so highly polished it looked liquid, and through a door that led to a cellar with a vaulted stone roof. The cellar was musty and damp, with a grayish mold growing on the walls. When she rubbed her bare arms to warm them against the cold, Khalid gallantly wrapped an arm about her, but she could feel a tautness in his grip.

"We age our wines in these small oak barrels," Aulestia told them, "because we believe it improves their quality."

Khalid's fingers rubbed her flesh in concentric circles, and she sensed that he was edgy. Surely there was no danger here. Uneasily, she recalled a news report showing Basque terrorists waging a gun-battle in a small village in the Pyrenees mountains. Were she and Khalid walking into a trap? Did these people provide armaments to both rebel and government forces alike? One of these days she'd file a story about the underground world of gun dealing.

Aulestia pointed to barrels as tall as she was, "Now those large old storage vats—but here, let my cellar master, Jules, explain what is going on. He is a trusted employee who knows everything. After your tour, you must come up to the wine room for a glass of our red table wine, the very best in Spain."

The cellar master, a man with a hooked nose and a paunch as big as a cask, barely acknowledged their presence. He continued to draw wine from a barrel with his pipette. When Aulestia was gone, Jules filled a silver tastevin from the pipette and passed the shallow tasting cup to her, saying, "First you check the wine's clarity and then, *señora*, you sniff it to check the bouquet, and finally you taste it."

While she followed his instructions, he turned to Khalid and said, "Señor, you will find the large storage vats excellent for shipping. Shall I arrange to have several sent to you?"

The almost indistinct grooves on either side of Khalid's sensuous mouth eased visibly. "I have friends on the island of Rhodes who would be highly interested in receiving several vats, say fifty. I assume the vats will contain your usual quality product?"

"Most certainly. You may make payments through our account in Zurich. Tell me, *señora*, how did you find the wine?"

So, it was that simple, the purchasing of arms. On the return trip to Rhodes she marveled more than once at the process. A mere exchange of certain key words acted as the open sesame. Fifty barrels—fifty tons of automatic weapons, explosives, ammunition, rifles, handguns, to be shipped out of San Sebastian.

As the sheikh's executive jet landed on the airstrip at Rhodes, she felt a shortness of breath that had nothing to do either with her consumption of cigarettes or the cabin's pressurization. Nor was it due to the nagging fear of the dangerous trip still to be made from Rhodes to the Macedonian coast. Her quickening pulse and shortened breath were due to the countdown of hours—minutes now—until she was in Damon's arms.

From her window she could not miss seeing her giant golden god. Then she saw the elegant blond woman with him, Lady Phillipa. A peculiar thudding hammered at her eardrums. Why, she was jealous! Such a miserable personality trait! Her innate, logical turn of mind reasoned that her competition for Damon's love was not a woman but a country. Nevertheless, her jealousy pounded away with nauseating persistence.

Next to her, Khalid said somewhat grudgingly, "This Damon, he is handsome, but he is too old for you."

She smiled thinly and said, "Khalid, I am a middle-aged woman who knows exactly what she's doing."

"But do you know exactly what you want?"

"Yes," she said firmly.

Damon and Lady Phillipa met them at the bottom of the steps, and Khalid's playboy good looks were diluted instantly in the presence of Damon's hard male vitality. Away from Damon, she had wondered if—no, hoped that—she had imbued him with a larger-than-life aura that he didn't really have. She was proven wrong. The almost physical possession of his gaze fired the blood in her veins, and she at once felt weak and flushed.

"Your trip was successful?" he asked her.

No words of love or affection, but the proprietary way his hand took her upper arm, withdrawing her from Khalid's care, was enough.

The diminishing roar of the jet's engines was almost deafening, so she merely nodded and let him lead her away, with Lady Phillipa and Khalid following.

A little later they drank coffee in the Lazeroses' tiny kitchen. Sotoris sat between her and Lady Phillipa, and Sophie was wedged next to Khalid. Due to the lack of space, Damon stood, his palms braced on the edge of the enameled sink, and fired questions at Khalid. Despite the Arab's nonchalant replies, she could tell that his male pride was bristling under the direct probing of the more experienced man.

"You are certain you know where and when the shipment will arrive and how to handle any trouble?" Damon pushed.

"Damn it!" Khalid snarled abruptly. He was half out of his seat. "Do you want to do business with us, or shall I notify my uncle to call off the deal?"

"Khalid," she said in an attempt to pacify the young man, since so much depended on the sheikh's goodwill, "it's just important that Damon knows exactly—"

Damon's hand, clamped calmingly on her shoulder, shut her up. "You're hotheaded, Khalid. Your uncle's generous terms are not worth jeopardizing the lives of our people. They are worth more to the PFF than weapons."

Khalid scowled belligerently at Damon's sharp rebuke, but prudently held his tongue.

Later, as she climbed the stairs with Damon to the rooftop, she said, "You're hard on the boy, Damon."

He caught her shoulders and turned her to face him. The starlight was cold on his face. "You are very naive if you think he is a boy, Sigourney. He is already half in love with you."

"And you?" she asked with a sad twist to her lips. She despised her weakness for asking him the eternal question of the lovelorn, but she could no more help herself than Khalid could.

His hands gently cupped her face. "I will answer you in the only way I can."

At his kiss, she arched against him like a black-haired cat, palsied by her yearning desire. His hands deserted her face to run over her body with caressing strokes, and she felt as if she were limned in fire.

His hands on her shoulders pressed her down, but when she would have pulled him atop her, he took control of her. He pushed her skirt and slip up about her waist. When he drew off her panties, the night air was cold on her bare skin. What he was about to do was an embarrassment to her, and she breathed, "Damon, no—"

But his hands anchored her wrists at either side of her hips. She tried to buck away, but his great strength subdued her. And then his warm tongue was stroking her furred flesh, and she gasped with the shock. Her head thrashed from side to side in refusal of the act, but gradually her body acknowledged what her modesty could not. She felt totally out of control. Her hips undulated with pleasure, and she could feel her own essence mingling with his saliva. A multitude of little explosions jerked her body in tiny electrical jolts, over and over.

At last, when she thought Damon would drain her of her very life, he mounted her with a strangled growl. Only then did she feel complete as she experienced the magic that could come only in her union with the man she loved.

He loved her through the night until the stars lost their race with the rushing dawn.

1. How do you rate _____
   (Please print book TITLE)

   1.6 ☐ excellent   .4 ☐ good   .2 ☐ not so good
   .5 ☐ very good   .3 ☐ fair   .1 ☐ poor

2. How likely are you to purchase another book:
   in this *series* ?   by this *author* ?
   2.1 ☐ definitely would purchase   3.1 ☐ definitely would purchase
   .2 ☐ probably would puchase   .2 ☐ probably would puchase
   .3 ☐ probably would not purchase   .3 ☐ probably would not purchase
   .4 ☐ definitely would not purchase   .4 ☐ definitely would not purchase

   T1

3. How does this book compare with similar books you usually read?
   4.1 ☐ far better than others   .2 ☐ better than others   .3 ☐ about the
   .4 ☐ not as good   .5 ☐ definitely not as good   same

4. Please check the statements you feel best describe this book.
   5. ☐ Easy to read   6. ☐ Too much violence/anger
   7. ☐ Realistic conflict   8. ☐ Wholesome/not too sexy
   9. ☐ Too sexy   10. ☐ Interesting characters
   11. ☐ Original plot   12. ☐ Especially romantic
   13. ☐ Not enough humor   14. ☐ Difficult to read
   15. ☐ Didn't like the subject   16. ☐ Good humor in story
   17. ☐ Too predictable   18. ☐ Not enough description of setting
   19. ☐ Believable characters   20. ☐ Fast paced
   21. ☐ Couldn't put the book down   22. ☐ Heroine too juvenile/weak/silly
   23. ☐ Made me feel good   24. ☐ Too many foreign/unfamiliar words
   25. ☐ Hero too dominating   26. ☐ Too wholesome/not sexy enough
   27. ☐ Not enough romance   28. ☐ Liked the setting
   29. ☐ Ideal hero   30. ☐ Heroine too independent
   31. ☐ Slow moving   32. ☐ Unrealistic conflict
   33. ☐ Not enough suspense   34. ☐ Sensuous/not too sexy
   35. ☐ Liked the subject   36. ☐ Too much description of setting

5. What *most* prompted you to buy this book?
   37. ☐ Read others in series   38. ☐ Title   39. ☐ Cover art
   40. ☐ Friend's recommendation   41. ☐ Author   42. ☐ In-store display
   43. ☐ TV, radio or magazine ad   44. ☐ Price   45. ☐ Story outline
   46. ☐ Ad inside other books   47. ☐ Other _____ (please specify)

6. Please indicate how many romance paperbacks you read in a month.
   48.1 ☐ 1 to 4   .2 ☐ 5 to 10   .3 ☐ 11 to 15   .4 ☐ more than 15

7. Please indicate your sex and age group.
   49.1 ☐ Male   50.1 ☐ under 15   .3 ☐ 25-34   .5 ☐ 50-64
   .2 ☐ Female   .2 ☐ 15-24   .4 ☐ 35-49   .6 ☐ 65 or older

8. Have you any additional comments about this book?

   _____ (51)

   _____ (53)

Thank you for completing and returning this questionnaire.
Printed in USA

NAME_____
(Please Print)

ADDRESS_____

CITY_____

ZIP CODE_____

BUSINESS REPLY MAIL

FIRST CLASS　　PERMIT NO. 70　　TEMPE, AZ.

POSTAGE WILL BE PAID BY ADDRESSEE

NATIONAL READER SURVEYS

2504 West Southern Avenue
Tempe, AZ　85282

Chapter 12

Agamemnon took the call. The muffled voice on the other end belonged to a VASIK contact, a *mafioso* out of Palermo. "I picked up her trail in northern Spain, at Burgos."

At last! After the long search, the woman had finally been tracked down. The general settled back in his leather chair, a feeling of pleasure that was almost sexual in its intensity settling over him.

"There's a problem, though," the muffled voice continued. "When she and that Arab drove up to Haro, a village near the Spanish Pyrenees—"

"Don't give me your song and dance routine," the general snapped. "I just want a status report."

"The Arab stayed too close to her for a clear shot. They left before I could pop her off."

Agamemnon ground out an obscenity, then drew a deep breath. "We do not need the unpleasant publicity she could generate. Do you understand me? Find her. She has to surface somewhere."

Agamemnon hung up the phone. The Hamilton bitch was still alive. But not for long.

"I take it that absence did not make the heart go yonder?" Father Murphy asked Sigourney the next morning, when she met him at Lindos quay. The priest had arrived on the sardine trawler to help in the arms distribution.

She slid her hands into the hip pockets of her jeans. "Alas, whoever came up with that, Father, is full of it—at least where Damon is concerned. He's a force in my life I can't explain. Without him..." She shrugged.

"Where is he now?"

"With our benefactor's nephew, who is also my protector; an Arab, no less. They're working out the final plans before the arrival of the wine casks." Even along the crowded, noisy seaport, she was careful not to allude in any way to the political front or its operations.

The old eyesore of a man dropped his voice and said, "Well, my child, you do need a protector. When I left the mainland the radio was broadcasting the news that the Macedonian Minister of Justice was offering a very generous reward for the whereabouts of the world-renowned journalist, Sigourney Hamilton. They are claiming to fear that she has been kidnapped. Imagine that, will you!"

She stepped around a puddle on the wharf. "I can imagine it all too well. Once she's secretly rescued from the evil clutches of the PFF, she will be royally entertained at Toridallos Military Prison."

"All is not lost," the priest consoled her in a low voice. "Patriotic feeling is running high in Macedonia, despite Agamemnon's curfews and crackdown on dissidents. Martial law hasn't prevented staged riots and sabotage throughout the country. Unfortunately, the strikes have caused a shortage of food and supplies in some towns, hurting the citizens more than they disrupt the government."

They left the little seaport behind and climbed a dusty road leading up into the hills. "Damon felt it would be better," she explained to the priest, "rather than for us all to converge on the Lazeroses and draw suspicion, if we met someplace else."

"But so far on foot?" the priest huffed.

"The rendezvous is perfect; you'll see," she promised. "Damon and Khalid will meet us there within half an hour."

At the brow of the hill she paused. Below nestled an amphitheater built in Roman times. Tiers of marble benches had been restored, and a rehearsal of Sophocles's *The Trachinian Maidens* was in progress in the orchestra pit, which a couple of millennia earlier had been simply a circular stone threshing floor. A few tourists occupied benches here and there.

She touched the priest's shoulder and said, "Damon told me that the acoustics are so marvelous that we can hear the actors, but they can't hear us."

On the opposite side she saw Damon and Khalid walking toward them along the columned ramp that surrounded the amphitheater. They might have been ordinary tourists. Well, not ordinary. Actually, far from it. They were both too good looking not to be noticed. One a dark angel, the other a golden god.

Suppressing the hot flush of excitement she felt whenever her beloved was near, she left Father Murphy and began striding, more eagerly than her dignity would have preferred, toward Damon.

From a rocky ledge the swarthy Sicilian held his breath. He'd seen the woman and the walruslike Catholic priest coming through the olive grove, where the gnarled and pruned limbs were almost bare with the approach of winter.

He screwed the silencer on his M-1 and trained the telescopic sight on the empty spot before a weather-corroded column that she would pass in a matter of seconds. Three quick, silent shots—the triangle composed of heart, a lung, the brain—assured certain, instantaneous death.

Just before Sigourney reached Damon and Khalid, some rubble shifted treacherously beneath her foot. Her arms flailed, and she went ignominiously sprawling, barely avoiding the sentinellike column. Simultaneously she heard, from only a fraction of an inch away, a sound like "pew, pew, pew," as the stone pavement splintered just beyond her fingertips.

With a shouted instruction to Khalid, Damon sprinted past her. Khalid hurled his body atop hers, and the air whooshed from her lungs.

"Khalid!" she wheezed. "What's going on?"

"Don't move," the Arab snapped.

She twisted beneath him, but he wouldn't let her up until minutes later, when Damon and Father Murphy returned.

Chagrined, she ignored Khalid's outstretched hand and scrambled to her feet, brushing the chalky dust from her clothing. Father Murphy's black attire was also splotched with white powder.

Her demand for an explanation died on her lips when she saw the weapons Damon carried—his knife, smeared crimson, in one hand and a strange-looking high-powered rifle in the other. Immediately she knew what had transpired.

Incredibly, the rehearsal continued in the orchestra pit down below, and the few tourists seemed either unaware of or uncaring about the reason for the scuffling that had occurred on the ramp above them.

Damon's glance passed over her quickly but thoroughly. His dark eyes were turbulent, the blue-black color of storm clouds. His expression was one of utter virulence. Apparently satisfied that she was unhurt, he said tersely, "Our cover has been blown. We are leaving the island. Now."

Only then did her cowardly legs collapse under her like a folding chair. Total and crushing terror crouched in her mind. As Damon carried her in his muscular arms, her pupils focused blankly on the fabric of the shirt he wore. He was speaking to her softly, reassuringly. Distantly she thought she heard the fury of her pounding heart.

But it was his.

There was very little room in the trawler's berth, not even enough for the two of them to lie comfortably side by side. It didn't matter, really. Brooding, Damon lay on his side, cradling his slender, fully dressed lover against his length. Her hysterical sobbing had ebbed into soft hiccoughing and, finally, the steady breathing of exhausted sleep. He knew she was undergoing what psychologists identified as Post Traumatic Stress Disorder, PTSD, a condition usually experienced by soldiers and more commonly called shell shock.

In the dark, his hand rhythmically stroked her tangled hair, while he sought to restore his usually stringent self-control.

Someone had tried to kill her! Someone had tried to assassinate Sigourney!

He wasn't surprised that they were trying to kill her. He *was* surprised by how much he cared for her. The realization that Sigourney had been shot at had loosed that primal part of him. He had known with absolute certainty that he would destroy the bastard who had tried to kill her or be killed himself.

To lose his self-discipline in a moment of savagery was stupid, and would have helped neither him nor her had he not been successful.

Sheikh Ibrahim Rajhi had been right: He was dangerous for her.

He felt her eyelashes fluttering against his cheek. She stirred in his arms and said, "Damon?"

"I am here."

"Where is the boat headed?"

"To the training camp. The others are coming by separate routes."

She was silent for a moment, and the only sound was the gentle groaning of the trawler's timbers as it rolled in the waves. He knew she was trying to make up her mind about something she wanted to say. He waited patiently. It was all he could do: to wait.

"I'm sorry," she said at last. "I wanted to be brave for you."

"I have not always been brave either," he told her, his voice muffled by her hair. He would tell her what he had never spoken of to another human being. It would be the only thing of himself he could give her.

"I learned during the two years I spent in solitary confinement that a human being is most capable of enduring suffering."

He sensed that she was listening intently, so he went on. "There are prisons and there are prisons. Each of them is a world in itself. A community with its own rules and its own rulers. Only in rare cases are the prison authorities the actual rulers of the institution. The ruling caste is invariably a small group of inmates who, to all intents and purposes, run the prison without much interference from the authorities.''

He paused, choosing his words carefully, then said, ''Upon arriving in Toridallos, I was fingerprinted and documented. I spent a total of twenty months in solitary confinement, in chains for the most part. It was the best part, let me assure you. During that time I heard the screams of tortured men. Later, I saw one prisoner go mad after being injected with drugs.''

He heard her catch her breath, but he continued. ''When I was released into the general ward, I encountered men who weren't worthy of the name. My size drew interest from the deviates among the prisoners. Once, in an unguarded moment, six of them attacked. I managed to fight them off. But the degradation, the dehumanization of that moment...

''After that, I survived only by willing myself elsewhere. In my mind I was not really living in prison. I lived off my memories, thinking about my youth...thinking about happier times. I noticed that older people held themselves together better in prison. They had more memories to live off of.''

Sigourney was weeping softly in his arms, and he gently kissed the tears from her cheek. Long moments passed, and after a while he sensed an alteration in her breathing. He knew she was coming out of the trauma but still feeling the physical and mental aftermath—and feeling that driving biological need he had once explained to her.

He sensed what was coming, and he could neither ignore nor refuse her. At that moment she needed him intensely, in that ultimate manner in which a man and a woman find solace together.

In the cramped space, she sat up and pushed her hair back from her passion-dazed face. He cast her a quizzical look, but before he could say anything, she lowered her face to the fork of his legs. She nuzzled the rough denim, inhaling deeply of his scent and exhaling deep, shuddering breaths.

"Sigourney, you don't know—"

"Please..."

They stared at each other through the darkness. She lowered her head again to make love to him. Only when he groaned and she could see he was in pain, did she unzip the jeans. He watched her wrap those long, lovely fingers around him, her hair swirling in and out of his vision.

Gently he cupped her face, letting her love him. He didn't force himself, but after a while he tugged her silken mass of hair, drawing her face back to his. He kissed her lips, her eyelids, her cheeks, with immeasurable tenderness, a quality he had thought he had lost forever. She made him feel young and innocent again.

They drifted with the waves, until he slowly removed her garments from her and fitted her onto him. She began to move first, slowly rotating her slender hips, adjusting herself to his rigidity. His hands cupped her breasts, kneading them with infinite gentleness, his fingers slowly twisting her swollen nipples.

The urge to mate was in him, a maddening lust, but there was something else, too. So much emotion was being loosed in him that he felt like crying. He had never experienced such feelings before.

She was so perfectly attuned to him that he suspected she sensed what he was going through. Her movements slowed gradually but sensually, and her whispered words of passion renewed his desire.

In the confinement of the tiny cabin, only the sound of their bodies moving together could be heard, until he shuddered and grunted violently, like a great mastiff with fever, and lay inert, still coupled with her.

Sometime later he disentangled himself from her lissome frame to spread a woolen blanket over her. His old rage began to churn in him at the sight of her, so naked and vulnerable. How long before he could find the words that would force her to leave?

Chapter 13

The National Museum's marble floors were polished enough to please even a Medici, and the rooms were crowded enough for an agent to make a drop without arousing suspicions. A perfect place to make contacts. Lady Phillipa and Damon wandered through the rooms of paintings, sculptures and other *objets d'art*, appearing to vigorously discuss the merits of each work.

Lady Phillipa, who years earlier had played the role of patroness to several gifted artists, was not a little surprised by Damon's knowledge of the fine arts. They halted in an alcove that featured the works of a Macedonian surrealist painter.

Damon dug his hands in the pockets of his tweed jacket and canted his head to study one painting, saying finally, "The composition is too crowded."

They were alone in the alcove, and there was no need to continue the charade of being a married couple, but she was unable to help herself. Her face impassioned, she lovingly touched his jaw with her fingertips.

"How long, Damon?" she whispered. "How long before Kopeta's VASIK closes in on you? Can't you see that sooner or later the odds are going to catch up with you? Your luck will run out."

"And what of yourself, Phillipa?" He captured her dainty hand in his large one and brushed his lips across her fingertips.

His gesture should have thrilled her, but she knew it was done in homage to her bravery and nothing more, nothing that could even faintly resemble passion. The worst of it was that she was certain he was aware of her feelings. He had too much sensitivity not to be. Nothing escaped his notice.

Did he also perceive that she was tired of playing the lady? She wanted to be bitchy, to demand of him the love he owed her. Why not admit it? She *was* a bitch in heat, panting after him, but, dear God, she loved him so.

The rest of her life yawned before her frighteningly, a future of seeking solace elsewhere in place of the man she would never, could never, have. At least, not the way she wanted. She saw herself in the not too distant future as the stereotyped foolish, aging matron, escorted by gigolos. She felt a little sorry for herself, and a little angry.

Mentally she shrugged. She would settle for whatever crumbs she could pick up—and do so with no regrets. At least this one choice was hers to make. She couldn't control what others might feel for her, but she could control her own responses.

"I've been in contact with the leaders of the various PFF units," she said briskly, businesslike once more. "They've put their squads on standby for the arms distribution. I'm on my way now to the training camp to tie up the last of the details with Major Veronos and the Arab, Khalid Rajhi."

The merest flicker of a grimace passed over Damon's face, but he said only, "I'll join the rest of you at the end of the week. A few officials in Agamemnon's cabinet might be willing to divulge certain information pertinent to the success of our project."

She swallowed her jealousy and offered, "Any message you want me to relay to Sigourney?"

A group of school children, led by a museum guide, rounded the corner, forcing an end to the discussion, and Damon said, "No."

She and Damon parted, with him bestowing the briefest of kisses on her love-starved lips. With melancholy in her eyes and a wistful curve of her lips, she watched him stride out of the building.

"Patriotism," Khalid grumbled over the watery camp coffee, "is the willingness to kill and to be killed for trivial reasons."

"I know, don't tell me," Father Murphy said. "Mohammed said that."

"No. I did."

"Ahh, then I have one for you, my son. 'Don't be humble; you're not that great.'"

Sigourney laughed. "And I know who said that." She pointed her coffee spoon at the priest. "Indira Gandhi."

"Wrong," the old priest chuckled in triumph. "Golda Meir."

Khalid glanced across the table at them. He resented their lack of gratitude. After his return from Spain with Sigourney, Damon had stripped him of his pride that first evening on Rhodes. He heartily disliked the blond giant, but here he was, busting his ass to coordinate the arrival of the weapons. He wanted the PFF leader to know just how well he had managed the project.

"More coffee, anyone?" Sigourney asked, rising from the table.

"Is that what I'm drinking?" Khalid growled.

She shrugged. "Suit yourself."

He watched as she walked across the mess hall. Dressed in faded jeans, her old blue plaid shirt rolled to the elbows, and with tennis shoes on, she still exuded an air of elegance. Her regal mien shouted of finishing school—of Rodeo Drive and the Pink Zone and Rue du Faubourg Saint Honoré. Hard to remember that, according to the stories he had heard, she had been a Korean waif.

Still, there were those extraordinary eyes that contained all the mystery and promise of a *houri* to remind a man that she was one of those legendary Amerasian beauties.

She seemed to have recovered from the scare at the amphitheater earlier that week, but there was a haunted look in her eyes that he didn't remember seeing before. He had convinced Damon to let his uncle put his own special investigation team on the sniping incident.

"It will mean involving more people than I like to," Damon had argued.

"It is my job to protect her! Don't you care about her—whether she lives or dies?"

The steely eyes had narrowed, and the big man had said, "She almost died there at the amphitheater. Were you able to protect her? No!"

Khalid knew that Damon Demetrios didn't suffer fools gladly. Still, he had continued to argue, and finally the Macedonian had relented. Soon Khalid hoped to have a report on the incident.

"Sigourney has a lovely spirit, doesn't she?" Father Murphy asked guilelessly.

Khalid shifted his gaze to the old priest's misshapen face, uncertain of his meaning. From their first introduction, he and the Catholic priest had circled each other warily, like dueling bantam roosters. "You are talking of the soul?" he asked suspiciously.

"I am talking of her dedication to Damon. Many men would give everything to be loved with such single-minded passion by a woman like Sigourney Hamilton."

"What does Damon give?" he sneered.

"My son, love doesn't ask, 'What will you give me in return?'"

"Now *you're* beginning to sound like Mohammed."

Khalid rose from the bench and headed for the door. One part of his mind was reviewing the system he and

Major Veronos had worked out for the weapons delivery and distribution, while another was vowing that he would yet charm Sigourney; he would make her appreciate him.

The sentries at the barbed-wire entry let him pass outside with only brief glances. The overcast day held the possibility of more rain, and he strode rapidly the three miles to the secluded cover where the consignment of wine barrels was to be smuggled ashore the next morning. They were to be stored in an abandoned limestone chapel in the woods until the arms could be dispersed to strategic areas in Macedonia itself.

The coordination and carry-through of any project took forethought and detailed planning. Planning, organization, coordination—they were his field of expertise, for which his uncle paid him handsomely.

This particular task meant taking time to examine and reexamine every small detail. He hoped to produce a dry run before the actual distribution began.

Meanwhile, Damon was somewhere in Constantine, obtaining by whatever magical means the man seemed to possess that week's time schedule for Macedonia's coastal patrol cutters. Khalid knew well enough that the possession of a schedule was no guarantee that it would be adhered to. Still, it was wise to take advantage of any information.

He stopped at the edge of the treeline, where scrubby growth claimed the land sloping down to the surf. Above the slapping sound of the breakers hitting the beach, he heard the faint purr of a motorboat.

As he stood stock still in the leafy shadows, he saw a sleek inboard swing toward the rotting wharf. When new, the boat must have cost a pretty penny. At the moment it looked like it could use some touching up.

A man wearing a skipper's jaunty billed cap and a navy pea coat jumped lightly to the wharf to loop the boat's mooring line over a piling. Then he helped a lady in a red blazer jacket and white sweater and trousers onto the pier. Khalid recognized her at once; it was the aristocratic woman who, with Damon, had met Sigourney and himself at the Rhodes airstrip—Lady Phillipa Fleming.

The woman said a few words to the man with her. He nodded several times before reboarding the motorboat. Khalid watched her wave as the man steered the craft back out to sea; then he stepped from the concealment of the foliage into view.

Lady Phillipa turned and spotted him. He saw how her delicate frame stiffened momentarily. At the Lazeroses she had spoken to him, but only with polite reserve. It didn't take a prophet to see that the woman was in love with Damon Demetrios.

She began to stroll toward him, her stride long and assured, but her chin was raised in a manner that gave her away to him. Instantly he knew she was wary—and possibly a bit intrigued by him. He recognized her body language. He had seen it often enough in would-be mistresses.

He dug his hands into his trouser pockets and said casually, "Do you always travel in such an expensive form of transportation?"

In order to reach the trail to the training camp, she had to pass by him. She looked up at him. "I do when I want to convince interested parties that I'm on a romantic holiday outing. Do I look like the sort of woman a date would take out in a sardine boat?"

He shook his head slowly and smiled. He couldn't have Sigourney, so he would beguile this woman. Older women always appealed to him, anyway. "No, you look like the sort who belongs on a sumptuous yacht."

She returned his smile, and he detected a gleam of speculation in her gaze. He noted that the networks of fine lines around her eyes and her mouth were softened by the clouds that filtered the sunlight. "Well, I'm afraid that craft was the best PFF could furnish for today's charade," she said.

He took her arm, and they started off on a leisurely stroll along the beach. She fell in easily beside him, as though they had planned a tryst. "Who's the gentleman on the motorboat?"

She laughed. "That gentleman is a carpenter and the father of five children, the grandfather of a new-born— and one of us. We've been meeting with contacts who will pick up the shipments targeted for the guerrilla brigades throughout the Rhodope Mountains."

"So, you're the one who got that assignment." He hadn't known just whom the major would pick to carry out the various tasks involved.

She flashed him an amused glance. "You seem too young to be involved in an operation like this."

His male ego recognized her statement as containing a possible insult, and the ends of his clipped mustache twitched with the slow smile that creased his dark, handsome features. "Gun-smuggling operations are just one of my areas of expertise."

The nippy wind tossed her short, stylishly cut hair, making her look much younger. The curls invited his fingers to ruffle them, and he gratified his desire. While his hands romped through the wind-rumpled curls, she stood very still, her lips slightly parted. His flashing Arab eyes slid to her heaving breasts, then back to her excited face. She closed her lids, her lightly mascaraed lashes quivering.

Without touching her body, he lowered his mouth to hers in an exploratory kiss. They stood like that, separated by inches, while their mouths asked and answered questions through the medium of their kiss. Excitement building in him, he clutched her against him. His tongue savaged the inside of her mouth fiercely, and she returned that ferocity, kiss for kiss.

For a moment his male ego exulted. Then his keen desert instinct told him that all was not as it should be. In his conceit, he had not considered that, as he was using her in place of Sigourney, Lady Phillipa was using him in place of Damon.

Lightly he grasped her shoulders and gently pushed her away. "We're quite a pair, Lady Phillipa."

She didn't try to pretend that she didn't understand his meaning. "Aren't we." There was a tiny melancholy curve to her lips.

Damon stood before the subway urinal. In the wall mirror the narrow face of the lanky man next to him was unfamiliar; however, the verbal exchange went as prescribed.

"They say the Aegean is rough this time of year," the man said. The statement was casual enough, but the man's pale eyes glanced nervously about the empty restroom.

Damon zipped his trousers and replied in an off-hand manner, "Oh, you could weather the seas in a proper boat. A cutter, maybe."

Unexpectedly the man turned and fled the little room, scattering the wadded paper towels littering the grimy floor. Before Damon had a chance to react, soldiers spilled through the doorway. He knew at once what was happening. The sight of Colonel Kopeta's Mongol face among the machine-gun wielding gendarmes confirmed his worst fears, nightmares he had never wanted to experience again.

Pleasure flitted across Kopeta's flat features. "At last, we meet, Demetrios."

Damon flashed a deliberate grin. "Attila the Hun, isn't it?"

Kopeta nodded at one of the soldiers, and the man jammed his rifle butt into Damon's stomach. He doubled over with the excruciating pain. The VASIK colonel had no sense of humor.

Damon remained calm, made no struggle while he was roughly handcuffed and shoved up the subway stairs. A few brave souls stopped to watch as he was thrust into the back of a black sedan that waited outside the subway exit.

On the ride to Toridallos Military Prison, he mentally prepared himself for the ordeal of the constant struggle to hold himself together as a person. Rather than let himself dwell on what awaited him, on the horrors of totally subhuman conditions, of cattle prods and other methods used by military intelligence to break political prisoners, he forced himself to reconstruct the events of the previous weeks.

How had he given himself away? Had his impassioned involvement with Sigourney made him less than cautious? His mind spun back to the conversation a day earlier at the museum with Phillipa. She had mentioned that his days were numbered. Had she known something? Could she have betrayed him?

He would have plenty to occupy his mind during the trials to come.

Chapter 14

As Khalid and Lady Phillipa made their way to the mess hall, the female officer called Melina stopped them and told Khalid that Major Veronos wanted him. The major paced his makeshift office, which didn't even have its own ceiling. Khalid noted the grim lines about the man's mouth and knew something was amiss. "What has happened?"

"Twenty minutes ago our wireless reported that a Macedonian navy cutter had intercepted and fired tracer bullets across the bow of a Cypriot-registered trawler."

"Was the trawler in territorial waters?" Khalid demanded.

"Just inside."

"*Wallahi!*" Khalid cursed lowly. His hand rubbed the bridge of his bladed nose. What could have gone wrong?

Could Macedonian Intelligence have been shadowing him and Sigourney from the time they—

"Khalid!"

He spun around. Sigourney stood in the office doorway. Against the sleek black frame of her hair, her face was as white as the sands of Oman. He stepped over to her, catching her upper arms to support her, and she sagged against him. "What is it, Sigourney?"

"Damon—it just came over the radio—Damon has been arrested!"

"Oh, God, no!" Lady Phillipa cried out behind him.

"That does it," he told Sigourney. "I'm getting you out of here. Macedonia's a veritable trap."

She tensed and withdrew her arms from his support. "No, I'm not leaving. Not without Damon."

Lady Phillipa, her face blanched with grief, came up to touch Sigourney's shoulder in a compassionate gesture. "Think, Sigourney. Do you really think Damon would leave Macedonia, even if he could?"

"She's right," Khalid said. Buried inside him a small ember caught spark; there was hope now. Sigourney could be his. "Your remaining here won't help Damon. You can do more for him in Dubai, or anywhere but here."

A nerve flickered in her cheek. She pushed between him and Lady Phillipa. "Major Veronos," she said, crossing the room to plant her palms on his desktop, "Damon is being held at the Toridallos Military Prison. How soon can a force be gathered to rescue him?"

The man rubbed his eyes that were shadowed with weariness. "I wouldn't put a dog in there."

"How soon?" she persisted.

At last he looked at her. "We cannot do anything about Damon, Miss Hamilton."

Sigourney straightened. Incredulity and uncertainty tensed her features. "What do you mean? What are you saying? You can't let an important man like Damon remain in there to be tortured and—"

Khalid knew she couldn't bring herself to admit what would inevitably happen to Damon.

"Miss Hamilton," the major said in a tired voice, "the force that it would take to rescue him—it would mean a good thirty to forty men. Agamemnon is preparing his military for another offensive strike, so we need every man; *every* man is important to us."

"As important as Damon?" she challenged in a seething voice. "Think what he knows!"

"Whatever he knows, the Macedonian Intelligence will never get it out of him."

A visible shudder rippled through her body. A freezing silence reigned in the little office. In each mind was a horrible image of the tortures Damon would undergo. The other three had in one way or another witnessed the cruelty of warfare. And Khalid knew very well the subtle tortures of which the Bedouin tribes were capable.

Sigourney whirled. In her pale, wrathful face, her eyes accused the other three. "All right! Damon is not important enough to risk rescuing. At least not to you. But he is to me! Somehow, some way, I'm going to get him out of Toridallos!''

Khalid replaced the telephone in its cradle and drummed his fingers on the booth's metal frame.

"Well?" Sigourney asked impatiently from the door.

"The Saudi lawyer advises that there will probably be no bail set for a political prisoner."

"One of his cellmates was released!"

Khalid sighed. "The man held Italian citizenship in addition to Macedonian. The Italian consul raised a stink."

With a grimace of frustration, she turned and looked out at the wintery gray sea. Boats of all kinds still rocked at anchor in Tipraeus harbor, but the Balkan shipyard was closed, since it was Sunday, which was all the better, because there would be less chance of their being noticed.

Her booted foot tapped nervously. Too vividly she conjured up the story Damon had told her of his two hellish years in Toridallos. A chilling sheet of ice froze her brain. She pivoted and said, "All right. I'm going in."

"In? In where?"

"Toridallos."

"Good God, Sigourney! Don't you think prison security will be on the alert for you!"

"Not if I pose as a relative or an old friend from his village."

He raised his palms. "Okay, all right. You might get in; you might even get out. But you'll never get Damon out with you."

"I'm going to try, Khalid."

He shook his head in wonder. "Your love for the man is astounding."

"Will you help me?"

"To make myself worthy in your eyes, Sigourney, I'd do many things, but this—this is insanity...."

Five of them sat in the Lazeroses' kitchen and made plans. The Lazeroses' two daughters played upstairs.

"Reconnaissance is to be the watchword," Khalid told the others—Sotoris, Sophie, Lady Phillipa and Sigourney. "We must be familiar with every inch of the escape route before we even embark on this madness."

He looked at Sigourney. "All right, do you remember what I told you to look for once you get inside?"

She nodded, her long hair swaying against her cheek. "Security, numbers of guards, weaponry, layout of the place, cover, high ground."

It was a long list, and he knew she was anxious to remember every detail of his instructions.

"Sotoris?" he asked. "What's your job?"

"Establish police presence," the man answered. "Check the mountain roads for clear passage. Make certain of gasoline caches along the way."

"Sophie?" Khalid asked next.

"I have located a vehicle in Constantine. It belongs to a wealthy left-wing member of Agamemnon's parliament." She smiled dryly. "Father Murphy is approaching the family now about contributing the Land Rover to the 'Protect the Animals' cause."

"I've arranged for another set of papers for Damon," Lady Phillipa said.

"Good. Also, get a photo of Agamemnon. It won't hurt to have it stuck on the windshield when we pass through Alexandros."

"Alexandros?" Sigourney asked. "That's the army's training center outside Constantine, isn't it?"

"If what the major told me is correct, yes. That would be the last direction Agamemnon's Intelligence would expect us to take."

Sotoris nodded slowly. "Absolutely dangerous—but a good idea."

"We'll need a change of clothing for Damon, too. He's a big man. Clothes that large will be hard to find."

"I'll find something for him," Lady Phillipa volunteered.

"Fine." Khalid's eyes lingered on her only momentarily. Lady Phillipa was no lady in bed. She made love to him as no whore ever had, and yet she was in love with Damon.

Toridallos Military Prison, in the northeast section of Constantine, was part of a larger military complex. On its west side was the old Sultan's Palace, which had been converted into a police academy by Agamemnon. The prison compound had once been the palace gardens. On the north side were military offices, including the draft registration office, and to the east were an armory and garrison and a landing pad where helicopters took off and landed daily.

The compound itself was bounded by an outer wall twenty-five or thirty feet high, and an inner wall fourteen feet high. Inside were fifteen or twenty separate buildings, including a laundry, a kitchen and cell blocks, one of which was reserved for women.

Sigourney had to find out which cellblock building housed Damon. She stood outside the steel door in the high brick wall and looked up at the gun towers on the walls—a formidable sight. A feeling of utter hopelessness clutched at her lungs, but Damon was close, somewhere just beyond, and she would find her beloved.

She and Khalid were pinning their hopes and plans on the usual red tape foul-ups of governments everywhere. Dressed as a peasant woman, with a woolen scarf tied over her knotted hair, she planned to slip in with a bunch of other visitors. In her arms she carried a box of groceries, warm clothing and books for Damon. She had wanted to include some kind of weapon, but Khalid had sternly forbidden it.

"Your job today is to assess the situation. That's all! Anyway, you can be sure they'd find whatever you tried to smuggle. Don't do anything foolish, Sigourney."

She glanced over her shoulder. Across the square a minor demonstration was taking place. Soon troops would arrive to disperse, by whatever means, the brave, and perhaps foolhardy, dissidents.

Diagonally across the square from her, Khalid sat astride one of the motor scooters everyone in Macedonia rode. In his black leather jacket he looked like a punk kid. He seemed to be flirting with the girl behind the pistachio cart—Melina, the major's one contribution to the rescue mission.

Should trouble arise, should Sigourney be recognized, Melina would create a diversion with her cart, while Khalid helped Sigourney escape. Implausible, maybe, but not altogether impossible.

Neither was Damon's liberation, and Sigourney tucked her chin into the collar of her dumpy coat and pushed her way through the crowd to the small window that was set into the brick wall beside the steel gate. From within, a guard could see everything going on outside.

She showed her papers and spoke the name of one of Damon's fellow inmates. The guard nodded, and she followed the visitors ahead of her through a Judas door set in one of the huge gates.

The door clanged shut behind her.

She had passed the point of no return.

She walked through a second pair of steel doors into the prison compound itself. It was an immense area, with actual streets running between the buildings. With the other visitors, mostly women, she passed through another doorway into a reception room and once again showed her papers. The clerk pointed to a register. When her turn came, she set down the box and signed her assumed name in an almost illegible scrawl. The clerk handed back her papers and waved her on.

She left the waiting room and returned to the prison compound. Building Eleven, the clerk had said. She started toward it, her heart beating louder by the second. Damon. Damon. Damon. Please be all right. She wouldn't let herself imagine what they could have done to him in the past week.

Building Eleven was three stories high. It was terribly cold inside, and the floors were slimy, so she walked very carefully.

The visitation room on the second floor looked just like similar rooms in prison movies she had seen, with a long counter dividing the room, and reinforced wire stretched from countertop to ceiling to prevent the passing of weapons or other illegal items. Armed guards manned both sides of the wire divider.

This time, she gave Damon's name and waited. Further down the counter an old woman glanced about nervously, wringing her veined hands as she waited to see a prisoner.

A barred door opened, and Damon, handcuffed, entered. Sigourney wanted to cry out. She bit back her words, stifled the tears choking her throat. He stood looking down at her, and she knew he didn't recognize her at first. For one thing, his eyelids were badly swollen and circled by purple and black bruises. His lips were puffy, too. But at least he was still alive!

He eased his great body into a chair, and she suspected that the rest of him was as bruised as his face. In his eyes she saw not terror but despair. Suddenly his lips compressed into an angry line, and she knew then that he had recognized her.

"What the hell are you doing here?" he asked in a gravelly mumble. Gone was the mellifluous baritone. From swallowing back screams of agony?

Tears formed at the corners of her eyes. She wanted desperately to touch him. "Damon," she whispered in a low sob, "it won't be long. We're going to get—"

"No!"

The nearest guard looked suspiciously over at them, and she ducked her head to lift the box at her feet. "Look, I have brought you some things. See, even a paperback copy of the *Odyssey*."

She slid the box over to the guard. While he rummaged through it, she said in French, her voice low, "You must give me an idea of the schedule here—when you eat, exercise time, bedtime, everything—anything—you can think of."

He rose awkwardly to his feet and nodded toward the guard. "Take her away."

"Damon!" she screamed out.

The old woman and the prisoner she was talking to—a man young enough to be her son—stared at Sigourney.

Oblivious to all else, she dug her fingers through the holes in the wire and wailed his name again, but he merely looked at her and turned away.

Then one of the guards clamped his hands on her shoulders and yanked her away from the wire. Hands over her face, weeping, she stumbled back the way she had come.

Chapter 15

Sigourney pointed out the locations of two more doors on the map of Toridallos that Khalid had hand-drawn. His jaws were stubbled with a two-day growth of beard, and his usually neat dress shirt was rumpled and his tie loosened.

"All right," he said. "Where are the guards stationed? And how many?"

"How many?" she asked dumbly, shoving away her tangled hair; she couldn't remember when she had last brushed it. "Ten. A hundred. An army. Oh God, I don't know!"

With a grimace he dropped the pencil onto the floor, where he sat cross-legged. "Okay, let's get some sleep. We'll do better in the morning."

She got up from the orange crate she had been sitting on and paced the fifteen steps over to the apartment door and back. She knew the shabby little apartment well; she had walked its perimeters often enough the past two days. It wasn't the same one she and Damon had shared. This apartment, even barer and more dilapidated, was located somewhere in a Constantine ghetto called Abolhasso.

She stopped before Khalid, who, in that cross-legged position, looked like he belonged on a Muslim prayer rug. He watched her carefully, like a prison psychotherapist. Did he think she was ready to break? Her hands twisted together. She didn't think she'd ever get warm again.

"There's no time to sleep, Khalid. It's been ten days now. Damon might not even be..."

She didn't let herself finish the sentence.

Khalid rose fluidly and captured her pale hands between his own. "It's just as well. I don't think I can sleep on a mattress with you another night."

She smiled wanly. "I'm sure it's my red eyes that have been tempting you from your sleep."

"No, Father Murphy's snoring."

She tried to manage a smile and couldn't. Hands knotted and teeth clenched, she shut her eyes, closing out the horror of what was happening. She was terrified. The only important thing in her life might be taken from her. How she yearned to feel his lips on her, reassuring her; his hands, so powerful and yet so gentle.

For a moment she almost felt as if what she had wished for and wanted so fervently had been granted. But the lips pressing against hers were not Damon's. For one all too brief second beneath the tenderness of the probing kiss, she willed herself to believe, let herself respond hungrily; she wanted desperately to believe once again in the magic of Midsummer Midnight.

At last, almost reluctantly, she opened her eyes. Khalid's velvet brown eyes searched her face with a lover's hope, "I'm sorry, Khalid," she whispered. "It's Damon I love."

"And if he doesn't want you?"

"I still belong to him."

"After this is over, if we rescue him from—"

"*When* we rescue him!"

"All right. After we rescue him, I'm taking you out of Macedonia with me. I can make you love me, Sigourney, if you let me."

She turned away, not wanting to think beyond the problem of getting Damon out of Toridallos. All her will and energy were directed toward that goal.

Khalid came up behind her and gripped her shoulders. "All right, Sigourney," he growled into her ear. "Damon's rescue will be my love gift to you."

At that moment, in the hallway, Father Murphy gave the prearranged password, and Khalid, his mouth taut beneath his mustache, opened the door to admit him.

The two men amused her. The grotesque Catholic priest juxtaposed with the handsome Mohammedan playboy. There could be no stranger combination. For her sake, they managed to tolerate each other.

The priest, both arms hugging bags of groceries, looked from Khalid to Sigourney. "From the glum expressions, I take it the rescue plan is foundering."

Khalid relieved the priest of one of the sacks. "There are more difficulties than we anticipated," he said, going over to place his sack on the scarred Formica table.

"Toridallos looks as formidable as the Bastille," she told the priest.

He lumbered over to the table and set down the other sack. "There must be more riots going on throughout the countryside. I tried to get a bag of sugar at the market, but there was a shortage—"

He stopped, his hand in the air, holding a tomato. "Did you say the Bastille, Sigourney?"

"Yes."

He looked at nothing in particular and absently juggled the tomato. After a moment he said, "If you remember your history, a mob stormed the Bastille."

Khalid's head swung toward the priest. Restrained excitement brightened his eyes. "I'm following your thinking, Father. But there are only seven of us. Seven does not a mob make."

Sigourney clapped her hands joyously. "He has it, Khalid! We have our mob! Look out the window. Look at all the disgruntled faces! Think what seven agitators strategically placed outside the prison could accomplish!"

"When something good happens," Khalid said dryly, "it's a miracle, and you should wonder what Allah is saving up for later."

"From the Koran?" Father Murphy asked.

"No. Me."

There were seven of them in the Land Rover—Sigourney, Father Murphy, the Lazeroses, Lady Phillipa, Melina and Khalid—packed like college kids into a telephone booth. They had left the Abolhasso ghetto early that morning. Frost filmed the Land Rover's windshield, and Sigourney knew it must have snowed the night before in the mountains. What if snow blocked the passes? First things first, she told herself. Get Damon out of prison!

As Khalid drove toward the northeast section of Constantine and the Toridallos Military Prison, he grilled the six cramped passengers relentlessly with last-minute questions.

"Everyone knows what they're to do, once we have Damon out of there? Father Murphy, you go with Sigourney and me, all right? Damon might need emergency attention."

"Right," the priest said, his voice muffled by Sigourney's headscarf.

"Sotoris, Sophie," Khalid continued, "you drive that vegetable truck in front of the main gate as soon as we have Damon with us."

Sophie laughed ruefully. "Have you ever seen an elephant crush a snake? That's what one of those army tanks will do to the vegetable truck."

"Maybe, but it will create a diversion and give us some time; that's all we can hope for."

He questioned Lady Phillipa next, and while they went over her part in the escape plan, Melina surreptitiously touched Sigourney's hand.

"No matter what should happen," she said in a low voice, "I want you to know I was wrong about you. You are not the soft American I thought. Not here." Her fingers tapped the center of her chest. "Inside, you are a valiant woman, I think."

Sigourney squeezed the other woman's hand. "Thank you, Melina, but I am terribly frightened right now."

"You do not think the rest of us are not?"

As usual, men and women were milling about outside Toridallos. Some were waiting for visiting hours, others were there to heckle the guards. Some were out of work, with nothing else to do. There was also the inevitable gaggle of political dissidents, some waving placards scrawled with anti-Agamemnon slogans.

Sigourney reassured herself that nothing was impossible.

The seven instigators dispersed throughout the crowd to take their prescribed places. Sigourney threaded her way close to the gates. Nearby, she saw Khalid moving toward the brick wall beside the gates, near the guard's barred glass window. That early in the day, the little room was still empty. All about her she could hear frustrated grumblings. The crowd was sullen and restless, lacking only a leader to set it aflame.

From somewhere toward the rear of the crowd came a shout, "Our friends—our family in there—they're prisoners of Agamemnon. We all are!" It was Father Murphy's gruff voice.

"Yeah!" someone else shouted. "What has Agamemnon done for us?" Sigourney didn't recognize that one.

"His soldiers killed my husband!" wailed an old woman not far from her.

There was some shuffling in the crowd. Another voice demanded, "Shall we stand around and wait for them to kill our mothers and fathers and friends?" That voice belonged to Sotoris. "Let's get them out of there. Now!"

Cheering erupted among the men and women. Then someone, Sigourney couldn't see who it was, raised a rifle into the air and fired it. That started the stampede.

Above her, guards fired indiscriminately into the mass of bellowing people. The shots seemed to enrage the crowd even more, and she felt herself being shoved closer to the closed gates. So near the wall there was little chance of being hit by rifle fire from above, but she was afraid she might end up trampled by the mob. She fought frantically to keep her balance.

She could feel the hysteria rising in her throat. What was happening was a replay of her nightmares, a replay of her childhood, and she could feel all over again the terror of the monstrous army tank rolling behind her, crushing everything in its path.

Somewhere at the back of her brain, from a part that was still thinking rationally, came a warning that she had to get control of herself, or she couldn't help Damon. Not if she succumbed to her terror.

From the corner of her eye she could see a World War I vintage truck easing through the mass of people, drawing nearer to the gate. Sophie was at the wheel. They were one step closer to freeing Damon.

The resistance from the gun towers on the walls was half-hearted. After a few minutes of scattered—and apparently ineffective, since no one seemed to have been hit—gunfire, the guards disappeared. More cheering went up from the people. The mob surged toward the locked gates. Someone fired a burst of bullets at the gates, trying to shoot them open.

Near her, a bewhiskered old man wielded a rusty marlinspike, but she knew it was going to take explosive to open those gates. The beginnings of panic wriggled in the bottom of her stomach. Would the riot collapse for want of tools?

She grabbed the marlinspike from the man, thrust her way to the grilled window set into the brickwork, and smashed the glass.

"Freedom! Freedom!" The chant went up from the crowd at the small success.

Khalid, who had been swept several yards away by the pushing crowd, worked his way back toward her and called, "Give me the spike!"

The men and women closest to the window made room for him and watched as he attacked the brickwork in which the iron bars were embedded. Four or five others joined in, trying to pry loose the bars with their hands, gunstocks and anything they could find. Soon the bars were dismantled. A teenage boy squirmed through the window and disappeared from view.

"Freedom!" The mob continued to shout in what seemed like thunder. "We want freedom!"

Behind her, the crowd was pushing and shoving, and she knew that if something didn't happen soon, the people at the front would be crushed against the walls. Then, suddenly, the teenager was pushing open the little door in the gates!

The mob swarmed past her, and she was borne with them like a leaf bobbing on a flood-swollen stream. The large steel gates were shoved open next. Already cellblocks were being opened, and the inmates poured out.

She had to locate Damon among eight thousand prisoners. He could be anywhere—in the exercise yard, transferred to another cellblock, in solitary confinement again. Oh, God, let her find him. Let him be alive!

Khalid located him first; miraculously, she saw them hobbling toward her, though it would have been almost impossible to miss Damon's great height. Khalid had the big man's arm strung about his neck. Damon's face was gray, and, despite his immense frame, he looked gaunt. And old. She ran to them and flung her arm around his waist to help support him. At her touch, he winced.

"What have they done to you?" she cried.

"Not now," he warned in that gravelly voice that wrenched her soul. Though he was barely conscious, he was still in control of her.

"Let's get out of here first," Khalid said.

And out of the city and past the road blocks and through the snowbound mountains to Damon's village, she thought with aching despair. It was going to be a long day. They would need a lot of little miracles from Khalid's Allah and Father Murphy's God.

A block from the prison gates, Father Murphy was ready with the Land Rover. She and Khalid managed to shove Damon onto the back seat; then they climbed in front beside Father Murphy, with Khalid driving.

At Constantine Square, another riot was in progress. On one corner a Renault burned, its windows smashed. Khalid plowed the Land Rover slowly through the surging mass of shouting people. The mob wanted to release their anger, and everything was fair game. The Land Rover would certainly draw attention.

When several rioters with homemade clubs halted the car by leaning over the hood, Sigourney forced the breath into her throat and smiled at the acne-scarred man who poked his head inside her window. When the man saw Father Murphy wedged between her and Khalid, he said, "Oh, sorry to stop you, Father."

After that the checkpoint at Alexandros, Macedonia's military training center, was, astoundingly, even easier, because Father Murphy simply explained to the soldiers that he was taking a dying man home to his family.

"We should have thought of that excuse earlier," Khalid grudgingly acknowledged, in tribute to the priest's quick thinking.

From there on it actually seemed to her that there was more oxygen in the air, that she could breathe more easily. She felt almost anesthetized, and she shook her head as if to clear it of a numbing drug.

Constantly she turned to check on Damon. Father Murphy had brought a blanket, and a thermos of coffee for the long day ahead of them. When Khalid stopped to refuel at midday in a partisan village, she nursed Damon. More coffee dribbled out of his slack mouth than he swallowed.

Blessedly, only a thin coating of snow lay over the treacherous mountain roads, and they reached Damon's village by nightfall. Apparently his parents had already been informed that they were coming, because they had a room ready for Damon, the one in which she had slept the final night of Midsummer Midnight Week.

While his father, Khalid and Father Murphy helped him into bed, his mother hurried away for bandages and antiseptic. "And warm water," Father Murphy called from the bedroom.

Sigourney stood helplessly at the door. She wanted to do something. Anything.

Damon's mother came back with a wicker tray holding first-aid supplies. The diminutive woman took pity on her and, pushing the tray toward her, said, "Here, take this to the Father. I still have to see to the warming of the water."

The three men were undressing Damon. Out of consideration for his father, she turned and, placing the tray on a low chest, busied herself cutting up strips of muslin bandages.

When Damon was naked and half-covered by a sheet, Father Murphy bent to examine him. "Damn it, Father!" he muttered in a suppressed groan.

Sigourney whirled to face the men. "What happened?"

"He fainted," the priest said.

"Will he be all right?" Of course, he would be. She'd get the best doctors in the world for him.

"Broken ribs, the fingers of his left hand have been smashed, semistarvation. Luckily for him, I am a quack doctor—and a crack priest. Between the two professions, we will save him."

Once the examination was over and Damon was bandaged, it was her turn. Everyone left the room and consigned Damon to her keeping. The Father had given him a mild sedative, and he seemed to be dozing.

With the warm water his mother provided, she gently washed the filth from his body. She cringed when she saw his mangled fingers. Tears streamed down her cheeks, and she fought to keep from sobbing aloud.

"Sigourney."

Her head jerked upright. She had thought he was asleep. "Yes?"

"What you did—you were very brave."

She sighed inwardly. Would she ever hear the three words she longed for from him. "I'm brave because of you, Damon. Because I love you."

But he was already asleep again and didn't hear her.

Through the long night, she sat next to the bed, hovering over him, listening anxiously for the sound of his breathing, much as a new mother does her infant's.

Sometimes she rested her head on the mattress, her lips close to his feverish flesh. She worried that he had contracted some horrible disease in the filth-encrusted prison, and through the night she periodically bathed his face and pulse points with cold water.

Toward dawn, his mother peeked in. "How is he?"

Sigourney raised her head from the mattress. "He's running a temperature, but I think it's dropped some in the last few hours."

"You must get some rest, child."

"Please, I know I won't be able to sleep. Let me stay with him."

"My son is a strong man; he will be all right with you to care for him," she said, and closed the door silently behind her.

Damon dressed quietly. Even the mild effort of tucking his shirttail into his jeans taxed his strength.

His eyes were drawn to the sleeping woman. Her sooty black hair spread across the wash-worn sheets like a finely woven tapestry. Even with the dark smudges beneath her eyes, her face was beautiful. Her palms lay open, like a trusting child's.

She had trusted him. Her love had created some marvel of a man that he couldn't be. He had tried. For three days he had let her cosset him, knowing it gave her great happiness. And once, only hours before, he had found pleasure in *her* arms.

Weak and exhausted as he was, he had still managed to enter her, to lose himself in her cleanliness and her sweet-smelling breath, to escape the horrors of Toridallos, to find oblivion from the past and the world waiting outside. But that world was still there—waiting.

With his good hand he picked up her hyacinth cashmere sweater from the foot of the bed and rubbed his jaw against its furry softness; then he slipped out of the bedroom and made his way to the kitchen. Outside it was still dark, but his father was already up and dressed, ready to go out to the fields. The older man had filled the cast iron stove with a fresh load of wood, and the kitchen glowed pink with the fire's warmth.

"Coffee, Damon?"

"I'll get it, father," he rasped. His throat was excruciatingly raw. "Where are Khalid and Father Murphy?" he asked, removing the carbon-blackened coffee urn from the stove top.

"They returned to Constantine last night. The Arab said to tell you that there was still the matter of the distribution of the arms shipment. That he and Father Murphy would return for you and Sigourney. And..."

"And?" Damon prompted. He propped himself against the door frame to conserve his strength.

The old man swallowed the rest of the coffee in his cup. "I do not know why I let your mother sleep late in the mornings. She makes much better coffee than I do."

"What was the rest of Khalid's message?"

"That once the arms were delivered, the deal was finished and he was leaving Macedonia—and taking Sigourney with him, if she would come."

The coffee burnt the roof of Damon's mouth. "You are right. You never could make coffee, father."

"That is all, Damon—nothing about Sigourney?"

Damon's eyes clashed with his father's, both men determined, unwilling to give ground, both so much alike. "The MPA's about to put the revolution into gear. I have to be there."

"And Sigourney? She has traveled the width and breadth of Europe for you, broken laws and risked her life for you."

"Not for me, father! For some idealized lover that I can never be."

"You are afraid to be that man. You are afraid to give of yourself again."

"I am what I am. I cannot change."

"You are courageous, my son, but you are too proud."

"And you are not, father?"

The old man tossed his head, nodding up in Greek fashion. "Yes, I am proud. But not too proud to admit that I love a woman and would do anything to keep her as mine."

Damon set his empty cup carefully on the table. His lips trembled. "As she once told a sheikh, father, she is her own woman."

Chapter 16

Damon drove back into Constantine by an indirect route, to avoid the worst of the riots. He was fighting his weakened constitution, still evidenced by the tight, tired lines around his mouth. Sigourney, who was sandwiched between him and Khalid, had offered to drive, but he'd refused. "If we should be recognized and pursued, I know the back roads and escape routes best."

She noticed queues at every gas station. Every once in a while they passed a burning car or a looted shop with its windows smashed. They were stopped briefly at a roadblock, but the military had its hands full just trying to maintain order, and could do only a cursory check.

Their plan was to stash the Land Rover in the suburban garage of an attaché from the French embassy. Father Murphy had learned that the attaché and his family had left the country two days before, and their house was deserted.

Nightfall blanketed the beleaguered city by the time they reached the section occupied mostly by foreign diplomats. "Embassy Row," it was called. It was quiet here, which made it hard to believe that a revolution was suffering its birth pangs elsewhere around the country—unless one noted the many shuttered windows of the residences leased by foreigners who had already fled Macedonia.

With the Land Rover's headlights turned off, so as not to draw attention, Damon pulled into the garage. Khalid quickly closed the door, and total darkness descended on the four. The moment had arrived that none of them had discussed, certainly not Damon. The moment when Sigourney would either leave Macedonia with Khalid, or go with Damon and Father Murphy to the grounds of the National Palace, now occupied by revolutionaries. Lady Phillipa and the Lazeroses were already there.

She wished desperately that she could see Damon's expression. If only she could find a hint there that he needed her. No, it would have to be more than a hint. She would have to know that he needed her beyond all else.

A match was struck, and she saw his powerfully masculine features above the flame as he lit his cigarette. For a second his dark gaze held hers in a ruthless challenge. He shook out the match and, his voice, sandpaper rough, said, "It's time to go."

So, he was forcing the choice on her. He would neither encourage her to go nor beg her to stay.

She wanted to strike out at him. He left her no pride. She wanted to cry, to really sob, to be held in his muscular arms once more. She would never see Damon again! That knowledge was a knife thrust, a searing pain she could actually feel in her very heart muscles.

Father Murphy cleared his throat. "I feel the sudden need of exercise. Perhaps a brisk walk about the neighborhood will clear my mind."

Khalid touched her arm in a proprietary gesture and said, "I'll be waiting outside."

"No," she told him, "what I have to say—" She broke off and turned blindly toward Damon. She didn't have many words left in her that could come out in a sedate, controlled voice. "Damon, I told you once that I loved you, but not enough to watch you die." Now she was grateful for the dark. It hid the agony etched on her face, but she could hear the catch in her voice and was disgusted with herself. "I'd beg you not to fight in the revolution if I thought it would do any good, but... So...good-bye, Damon."

The crackle of rifle fire exploded closer this time, only a few blocks away from the Regency Hotel. From the fourteenth-floor windows, Sigourney could see the lights of the entire city. It was much the same scene she had viewed not so long ago, except the pinpoints of leaping flames scattered about Constantine were not bonfires this time but burning buildings.

The revolution had finally begun. The city was a power vacuum, ripe for anarchy. Could Damon and his PFF salvage something from the approaching collapse of the government that had created a severely brutal police state? And what about afterward? There would still be the Macedonian Provisional Army to pacify. Their radicalism could be as dangerous as Agamemnon's. If Damon were to survive...If Damon survived, she knew he faced a tremendous task in rebuilding Macedonia.

And the odds were against his survival. That she knew in her heart of hearts.

She turned away from the window and went back to the vast sitting room to find a cigarette. God, she was nervous. Where was Khalid? He should be back from the airport by now. What if he had been attacked by one of the roving bands of looters—or worse, arrested?

She finally found a pack of cigarettes in the bathroom, which was big enough for a cocktail party. She was living like a queen in a disintegrating city. Only a few guests still occupied the hotel. With the city in chaos, Agamemnon's iron grip was rapidly slipping.

Cigarette in hand, she went back into the sitting room and once more checked through her meager luggage, just enough clothing and other personal belongings to pass her off as one of the last tourists fleeing the war-torn capital.

Khalid had registered her in the hotel under the name of one of his uncle's wives—for whom she could certainly pass with her exotic looks—arranged a passport, and requested a suite at the front of the hotel.

"This way you can see the hotel forecourt," he explained. "If a squad of soldiers or a revolutionary mob storms the building, you will have plenty of warning. Besides the fire exits for escape, there are plenty of vacant rooms to hide in. This whole floor is empty. You're as safe here as anywhere else at the moment, but I'll be back in only a matter of hours—as soon as I can get reservations on the next flight out, whenever that may be."

Then his hands were on her shoulders, and he hugged her against him, his eyes dark with unfulfilled passion. "Unless it becomes imperative, don't leave your room. Don't even show your face. Do you understand, sweetheart?"

Had he been afraid she would change her mind and still go to Damon? Now that she was actually, finally, leaving the one and only man she had ever loved, she would have thought that her soul would be shriveling inside with her despair. But that wasn't the case at all.

She supposed she was one of those neurotics who recover their health and even their serenity when real disaster finally strikes.

The day would surely come when she would hear of Damon's death. She could only hope that by then a glacier would have settled over her feelings. Never again did she want to know what it was to truly love.

In the corridor she heard the elevator doors open and close. She froze. It could be anyone. Why hadn't she kept watch over the hotel forecourt?

"Sigourney?"

Khalid! She unlocked the door and threw her arms about him. "I was so afraid something had happened to you!"

He looked down at her, his mouth curving triumphantly beneath the sweep of his mustache. "You do care for me!"

"Of course," she said lightly. "Who could resist a desert sheikh? A wealthy desert sheikh," she amended.

"Well, this wealthy desert sheikh had to pay a slight fortune in bribes to get a seat on the next flight out."

"Why?"

"Because it's also the last flight out. All the foreigners residing here—as well as a lot of the nationals—are scrambling for tickets. I've already checked us out of the hotel."

"The flight's leaving soon?"

He picked up their suitcases. "No one knows for sure. Olympia Airlines has shut down, but the United States has supposedly arranged for a special flight sometime before dawn—a Pan American 747 that leaves for Washington via Lisbon."

The streets were full of soldiers and tanks, but they were doing little to maintain order, much less control the congested traffic.

At an intersection the traffic had been stopped by people dancing in the streets. The taxi driver rolled down his window to shake an obligatory fist, and one of the revelers shouted back, "Agamemnon's dead! Hung by his heels!"

With a grunt Khalid said, "Now begins the struggle for control of the government's reins between the MPA and the VASIK. Between the two extremes, Damon will have his hands full."

The airport was bedlam. Their taxi couldn't get close to the service drive, which was jammed with cars, some abandoned by panicky drivers, so she and Khalid walked four blocks to the terminal.

Inside, fear tensed the faces of harried passengers, most of them from the diplomatic corps, waiting on tenterhooks for the arrival of the promised jumbo jet.

Those with families looked the most harassed. Their children, tired of the waiting, ran and shouted and played hide and seek among the rows of modernistic seats. Each businessman or foreign service executive secretly worried whether he would get enough seats for his entire family—or whether they might all be left behind.

The Olympia counter was unmanned, and a sign had been erected which declared that the airline was shut down until further notice. The departures board only said, *Delayed*.

At the Pan Am counter, people shouted and pushed, reminding Sigourney of what Wall Street must have looked like the day the stock market collapsed.

At a booth Khalid paid the small sum for airport tax, and then they made their way to the departure lounge. There the waiting began again. Her icy calmness began to thaw, helped along by smoldering embers of worry. The plane would fail to arrive; the passport control desk would question her papers; Kopeta's Intelligence had picked up her trail; they were coming for her and would take her away to that hellhole of a prison. But, no, the revolutionaries controlled Toridallos now, along with the National Palace and several other strategic areas.

She asked Khalid for a cigarette. Dinnertime had long since passed, and midnight was drawing near. She tried to read part of a two-day old newspaper that had been left in the chair next to her, but the news was so censored that it was like reading a fairy tale.

Now it was three o'clock, and the flight still had not been called. Khalid brought her a Styrofoam cup of coffee he had managed to get from God-knew-where. Even in that hour of crisis, her beauty drew appreciative, though distracted, stares from the terminal's edgy male passengers.

She smoked yet another cigarette and walked tight circles on the terminal's mosaic tiled floor. Damon had helped to design this building, this very airport. Damon. She would never see him alive again.

And the others, her comrades in arms, what would happen to them? Lady Phillipa and Sophie and Sotoris and Father Murphy? It was at this terminal that she had first bumped into the priest in what seemed a lifetime ago. So much had happened to her since then. She wished she had had the time to tell that ugly old saint good-bye, to tell Father Murphy just how much he meant to her. She wished—

"Our flight's been called!" Khalid said. He took her elbow and steered her toward the "Passengers Only" gate. The passengers were being taken by seat number, and fortunately, Khalid had obtained reservations in the first batch of thirty called, assuring them a place.

At the passport control desk, he handed the uniformed girl Sigourney's false passport and yellow exit form.

"Where are your papers?" Sigourney whispered to him. Dear God, don't let him have lost his ID now, she prayed.

The girl stamped Sigourney's papers without even checking them and returned them to her. "Your papers, sir?"

Khalid ignored her and looked at Sigourney. His mustache dipped with his wry smile, but his liquid brown eyes were solemn. "I fear the worst has happened, Sigourney, my love."

"What?" she breathed. "What are you talking about?" The girl was looking at both of them curiously, waiting. Behind them, the other passengers were getting restive. A baby wailed, and a little girl chanted a nursery rhyme aloud, getting on Sigourney's nerves.

"I fear I have become one of those abominable wretches known as a patriot. I'm not leaving."

"You're what?"

He shrugged. "I guess I have grown bored with my playboy status." He preened the lapels of his coat mockingly and said, "I think being a freedom fighter better suits my image. My uncle would approve, don't you think?"

She grinned, then started laughing, ignoring the gaping people. "I couldn't agree with you more," she said when at last she caught her breath.

Getting past the armed revolutionaries that guarded the National Palace gates looked impossible. The winter wind was freezing, but Sigourney would not be turned away. Blinking against the bright searchlights trained on the gate, she infused her voice with authority and demanded, "We want to be taken to the PFF leader, Damon Demetrios."

Finally she and Khalid were escorted by three revolutionaries wearing yellow armbands along the lengthy tree-lined drive into the great columned building. Within the marble-walled vestibule, there was another checkpoint to pass before they were ushered down a long corridor.

A man loped by them and shouted, "Colonel Kopeta—he's been assassinated!"

The closer they drew to the office commandeered by Damon, the more difficult it became for her to breathe normally. She warned herself that, in remaining with him, she would have to share him with Macedonia. She could expect nothing more of him than that. She consoled herself in the knowledge that they would have the common goal of a free Macedonia, something he had not shared with his wife. It would be something that could fuse their love into an unbreakable bond.

They encountered Father Murphy as he was leaving Damon's office. A positively beatific smile lit up his face, lending his grotesque features an almost unearthly beauty. "You're not leaving him! God bless you, child. He needs you, you know."

"No, I don't know that, Father. But I do know that I love him beyond anything."

She put her hand on the doorknob, and Khalid, laying a companionable arm across the priest's shoulder, said, "Father, did you ever hear the quotation, 'Forgive your enemies, but don't forget their names'?"

"Shakespeare?" the Father guessed, trudging off arm in arm down the corridor with the Arab.

"I don't remember, really," Khalid was saying. "I thought you might."

"No. But, say, have you heard, 'The man who...'"

Their voices were lost to Sigourney as she let herself into the office. She closed the door behind her, leaning against it to support her rubbery legs. The big Macedonian standing at the night-darkened window turned to face her. His usually impassive features betrayed his surprise; the turbulence of agony was carved there before he willed them into a mask again.

She tried to speak, but her throat was sealed shut with the burden of her love.

Slowly Damon walked around the desk and came up to her. His eyes, those brilliant blue mirrors of his emotions, moved over her face feature by feature, as if comparing what he saw now to what had been stored in his memory.

"Say something, damn you, Damon," she begged in a raw whisper. "At least say you're glad I came back."

"Sigourney!" Her name was a strangled groan. He sank to his knees before her and captured her palms, pressing them to his lips. Astonished, she felt his tears. His massive shoulders shook. Haltingly, he said, "I tried to deny the love I felt for you. I told myself that I had loved once. That that was enough. That now the only feelings I had a right to were those for my country. But I never loved as I have loved you!''

Tears welled in her own eyes. She had despaired of ever hearing such an admission from this man. Because she loved him so deeply, she had fortified herself to be content with being a part of his life in any way he would let her. He was her man, and it would have had to be enough. She knew now that most people never get the chance to experience this depth of love. Frightened by the vulnerability engendered by such a love, people go through life bestowing only the most superficial feelings on their partners.

She wanted to tell Damon this, but when she tried to move away he held her firmly, his arms around her hips, his head tilted back to look at her with glistening eyes. ''Sigourney, you must understand how much you mean to me! I realized, when I thought you had left Macedonia for good, that I was losing something most men hunt for all their lives. The feeling...All I can say is that the thought of losing you was worse than anything I suffered in prison. The past twenty-four hours have been a living hell for me. I love you, Sigourney, and I need you. You are a part of me. You have invaded my soul, my mind, my heart, taking up all the empty space so that I am only half a man without you. You must never leave me.''

She squeezed her eyes shut and hugged his glorious golden head against her belly. ''Never, Damon, my darling. Never will I leave you.''

Author's Note

Midsummer Midnight is purely a work of fiction. Macedonia as a nation ceased to exist centuries ago, divided up among Greece and some of its adjacent, now mostly communist-backed, neighbors. Regardless, there do exist freedom fighters like Damon and Sigourney. Married by Father Murphy soon after Agamemnon's downfall, they know, as their children do, that peace, like true love, can never be compromised.

READERS' COMMENTS ON SILHOUETTE INTIMATE MOMENTS:

"About a month ago a friend loaned me my first Silhouette. I was thoroughly surprised as well as totally addicted. Last week I read a Silhouette Intimate Moments and I was even more pleased. They are the best romance series novels I have ever read. They give much more depth to the plot, characters, and the story is fundamentally realistic. They incorporate tasteful sex scenes, which is a must, especially in the 1980's. I only hope you can publish them fast enough."

S.B.*, Lees Summit, MO

"After noticing the attractive covers on the new line of Silhouette Intimate Moments, I decided to read the inside and discovered that this new line was more in the line of books that I like to read. I do want to say I enjoyed the books because they are so realistic and a lot more truthful than so many romance books today."

J.C., Onekama, MI

"I would like to compliment you on your books. I will continue to purchase all of the Silhouette Intimate Moments. They are your best line of books that I have had the pleasure of reading."

S.M., Billings, MT

*names available on request

If you're ready for a more sensual, more provocative reading experience...

We'll send you **4** Silhouette Desire novels

FREE...

and without obligation

Then, we'll send you six more Silhouette Desire® novels to preview every month for 15 days with absolutely no obligation!

When you decide to keep them, you pay just $1.95 each ($2.25, in Canada), *with no shipping, handling, or additional charges of any kind!*

Silhouette Desire novels are not for everyone. They are written especially for the woman who wants a more satisfying, more deeply involving reading experience.

Silhouette Desire novels take you *beyond* the others and offer real-life drama and romance of successful women in charge of their lives. You'll share

precious, private moments and secret dreams…
experience every whispered word of love, every
ardent touch, every passionate heartbeat.

As a home subscriber, you will also receive FREE,
a subscription to the Silhouette Books Newsletter as
long as you remain a member. Each issue is filled
with news on upcoming titles, interviews with
your favorite authors, even their favorite recipes.

And, the first 4 Silhouette Books are absolutely
FREE and without obligation, yours to keep! What
could be easier…and where else could you find
such a satisfying reading experience?

To get your free books, fill out and return the cou-
pon today!

Silhouette ✦ Desire®

Silhouette Books, 120 Brighton Rd., P.O. Box 5084, Clifton, NJ 07015-5084

Silhouette Intimate Moments

COMING NEXT MONTH

A HANDFUL OF HEAVEN
Mary Lynn Baxter
Raine Michaels was sensible enough to know that falling in love with a pilot meant living with fear. But when she met Ashe her heart grew wings, and good sense flew out the window.

NIGHT MOVES
Heather Graham Pozzessere
Bryn's young nephew had been kidnapped, and there was only one man she could turn to for help: Lee Condor, the man she had pushed away in order to protect her heart.

CRITIC'S CHOICE
Sue Ellen Cole
Film critic Vea Valdez was always outspoken in her opinions. She had always denigrated Rafe Dougin's movies, but that was before her own heart started telling her there was definitely something wonderful about this man.

LED ASTRAY
Erin St. Claire
Cage Hendren was too wild for a woman like Jenny Fletcher, or so she thought...until he showed her that she, too, had a wild side, one that only he could tame.

AVAILABLE NOW:

MIDSUMMER MIDNIGHT
Parris Afton Bonds

NINA'S SONG
Anna James

BOUNDARY LINES
Nora Roberts

STAR RISE
Pat Wallace